Praise for Karen Kay and *Fairy Whispering*

'Karen Kay not only believes in magic – she creates magic. She believes in faeries and nature spirits, and she believes in the enchantment that happens when people come together to celebrate their love of the faerie realms, and how we as humans can interact with them. Karen Kay is truly a faery queen!'

WENDY AND BRIAN FROUD, AUTHORS OF
BRIAN FROUD'S FAERIES' TALES

'Karen Kay is one of the most magical people I know – I love to be in her presence because she brings so much light and joy. This book a wonderful tool for those who are curious about the hidden realms and how they can infuse their day-to-day life with magic, love, joy and fun. A must-read for anyone who is ready to let go, play and discover the brightest version of themselves.'

KYLE GRAY, BESTSELLING AUTHOR OF *RAISE YOUR VIBRATION*

'Karen's genuine connection to the fairy realm makes this a fascinating and change-making read. Explore her world, and this book, to discover the magic of fairies for yourself... if you dare!'

YASMIN BOLAND, BESTSELLING AUTHOR OF *MOONOLOGY*™

Fairy
Whispering

Also by Karen Kay

<u>Oracle Card Decks</u>

Pocket Oracle of the Fairies (2024)

Manifesting with the Fairies (2023)

Messages from the Mermaids (2020)

Oracle of the Fairies (2019)

<u>Audio Visualizations available on the</u> <u>*Empower You Unlimited Audio* app</u>

Manifesting with the Fairies Meditations (2023)

Elemental Meditation to Heal the Planet (2021)

Relaxation Meditation with the Mermaids (2021)

Rainbow Meditation for Relaxation and Peace (2021)

Star Visualization to Co-Create with the Universe (2021)

Unicorn Healing Meditation (2021)

Fairy Whispering

111

**Magical Practices for
Connecting with the Fairies**

KAREN KAY

HAY HOUSE

Carlsbad, California • New York City
London • Sydney • New Delhi

Published in the United Kingdom by:
Hay House UK Ltd, The Sixth Floor, Watson House, 54 Baker Street,
London W1U 7BU; Tel: +44 (0)20 3927 7290; www.hayhouse.co.uk

Published in the United States of America by:
Hay House LLC, PO Box 5100, Carlsbad, CA 92018-5100
Tel: (1) 760 431 7695 or (800) 654 5126; www.hayhouse.com

Published in Australia by:
Hay House Australia Publishing Pty Ltd, 18/36 Ralph St, Alexandria NSW 2015
Tel: (61) 2 9669 4299; www.hayhouse.com.au

Published in India by:
Hay House Publishers (India) Pvt Ltd, Muskaan Complex, Plot No.3,
B-2, Vasant Kunj, New Delhi 110 070; Tel: (91) 11 4176 1620; www.hayhouse.co.in

Text © Karen Kay, 2024

The moral rights of the author have been asserted.

The information given in this book should not be treated as a substitute for professional medical advice; always consult a medical practitioner. Any use of information in this book is at the reader's discretion and risk. Neither the author nor the publisher can be held responsible for any loss, claim or damage arising out of the use, or misuse, of the suggestions made, the failure to take medical advice or for any material on third-party websites.

A catalogue record for this book is available from the British Library.

Tradepaper ISBN: 978-1-4019-8026-9
E-book ISBN: 978-1-83782-331-4
Audiobook ISBN: 978-1-83782-330-7

Interior images: pp. 35, 45, 81, 111, 143, 179, 219, 239, 267 © Bonnie Helen Hawkins; all other illustrations Shutterstock

10 9 8 7 6 5 4 3 2 1

Printed in the United States of America

This product uses responsibly sourced papers and/or recycled materials. For more information, see www.hayhouse.com.

For my grandmother, Christabel Ellen Delamare.
Thank you for opening the fairy door for me.

Contents

Contents

Contents

Contents

Foreword

Brian and I are often asked if we really believe in faeries – if we honestly believe that there are other beings living in a world alongside our own, who are willing to interact with us, help us, guide us and enrich our lives. Well, the simple answer is yes, we do. Brian often says to people who are sceptical, 'Close your eyes for a moment and just pretend that you believe. Now, how do you feel?' Invariably, people open their eyes and smile – believing in faeries makes us SO much happier and more fulfilled than not believing.

As a small child, I was entranced by the idea of faeries. My mother was a firm believer: She read fairy stories to me from many lands and cultures, and together we made houses for the faeries in our garden, sang songs to them, left them notes and wrapped crayon drawings up in leaves for them to find. We did all of this with the total belief that the faeries were living alongside us, just out of sight but never out of mind. They were there to help us, guide us and play with us, as long as we respected them and, most of all, believed in them. We did. I still do and I always will. And along with that deep and unshakable belief in faeries is an equally deep and unshakable belief in the preciousness of the world around us, and an absolute need to respect and protect it for humans and faeries alike.

For Brian and myself, passing this belief on to whoever we can has become the focus of our lives. We do this by writing and creating art, in both two and three dimensions, of beings from the otherworld. Because we both feel a true connection with that world and its inhabitants, they seem to be forever eager to show themselves to us and to let us draw them into the human world through our art and creative endeavours. Because we believe in them, they are willing to show themselves to us and trust that we'll treat them with respect and love – which, hopefully, we always do!

You wouldn't have picked up this book if you didn't want to connect with the faeries or were at least curious enough to find out more about them. Here, you'll find a veritable treasure trove of inspiration and ideas for contacting the faerie world. With 111 ways to choose from, you can comfortably and easily communicate with the faeries in whatever way appeals to you the most. You are sure to find a way that feels perfect for you!

Many of these methods are very familiar to me and Brian – the book includes exercises and meditations we often do before we start a new venture or when we need extra inspiration – but we have also found new and interesting ways that we wouldn't have considered until reading about them here. Karen has come up with many we will try – maybe just for the fun of it and maybe to see if beings we haven't communicated with so far decide that the time is right!

The otherworld is infinite and the beings that inhabit it are infinite as well. We look forward to exploring this world in ever greater depth and reporting back on the new discoveries we make. We thank Karen for her ideas, for the playfulness she brings to the search for faeries and, above all, for her constant, delightful and unwavering belief in faeries!

For those of you who decide to explore and communicate with these beings, we wish you rewarding, world-expanding and beautiful experiences that you will continue to have for many years. Approach this with an open, playful and loving heart and oh, the wonders you will encounter! When you set off to find Fairyland, put this book in your travel bag – it's an essential and practical guide to discovering the shimmering enchantments of the faerie world. Travel safely.

Brian and Wendy Froud
Faerie explorers and documenters

Introduction

As children, many of us experience fairies, whether through fairy tales, art books, enchanting experiences or the whispers of fairies in our dreams or waking realities. As we grow up, this magic can fade for many of us. But what if fairies and magic are indeed very real, and all we need to do to reconnect with these enchanting realms is open our hearts and our minds? What if believing is seeing, rather than the other way around?

Chances are, if you're holding this book in your hands, you have a deep desire or yearning to hear the whispers of the fairies in your daily life. A desire to bring those beautiful childhood memories into adulthood. A yearning to remember that magic does indeed exist and fairies are just as much a part of this world as we are.

This book contains 111 ways to connect with the fairies through magical practices, including rituals, spells, meditations, incantations, visualizations and more. Ranging from the most simple to the complex, my wish is that you will use these practices to forge your own connection with the fairies in the best possible way for you, for the fairies – and, of course, for our beautiful planet.

When working or playing with fairies, there are no absolute rules, as everything in the fairy world is inside out, upside down, back to front, betwixt and between and topsy-turvy. If there's one thing you can be sure about, though, it's that you should always expect the unexpected!

The most important advice I can give you is to always be respectful, show your love and passion for nature, follow your heart and stay true. The fairy path is not for everyone – it requires an open mind and an open heart, and a sense of magic and wonder.

My name is Karen Kay and I have been hearing the whisperings of the fairies since I was a young child. It all started in my grandmother's garden. She was an avid gardener who loved roses. The beautiful, wild and natural fragrance of those flowers stays with me to this day, along with those magical childhood memories.

As a little girl, I would gather up the fallen petals as my grandmother pruned her roses. I would place them into a bowl, add some water, crush the petals, and *voilà*! I had made perfume for the flower fairies! It was, in reality, rose-water. However, to my innocent heart it was perfume and I knew that the fairies would love it! I would leave this fairy perfume out overnight in the tiny liminal space between two garages.

Then I would check on it the following day and it would always be gone. I knew the fairies had taken it, and that they appreciated my innocent gift.

I would also perceive fairies as tiny points of vibrant light, usually out of the corner of my eye. These fairy lights would appear in many different colours and would dart around, as if piercing through from the fairy realm into this human realm. I still see these magical fairy lights today.

I am often asked, 'How can I see or connect with fairies?' and now feels like the right time to share some of the secrets. I share from personal experience. Some of my suggestions may differ from those given in other writings about fairies. All I can say is that I share what is true for me, having worked and played with the fairies for more than 50 years.

Fairies are guardians of nature. They are here to oversee and nurture the flowers, plants, trees, rocks and crystals. Every living thing in nature has a fairy being close by, protecting it and encouraging it to grow.

A beautiful bonus of connecting with fairies is that they are magical. They can shapeshift and literally manifest miracles. We must never expect this though, and when we wish (which the fairies are happy for us to do), it must always be from our hearts and for the highest good of all.

Fairies are playful and have egos – in some ways similar to human egos, but in other ways different. Their playfulness can

3

sometimes be interpreted as mischievousness or naughtiness. Always trust your gut instinct and intuition when working and playing with fairies. The best way I can describe it is like this: In life, we meet many people – some people we like instantly and others... well, we are not so sure. Fairies are like people in this respect – we will not resonate with every fairy being, and vice versa. As is the way with people, fairies have individual personalities and there are nice and not-so-nice fairies! So, discernment is required when establishing a relationship with the fairies.

Fairy types, names and spellings

There are many names and various spellings for fairies, including fair folk, good folk, wee folk, little people, nature spirits, the fae or fey, faeries, faery, fayerie, pixies, sprites, nymphs, brownies, sídhe (pronounced *shee*), sylphs... the list goes on. Fairies are sometimes referred to as Earth angels or nature's angels, but let's clear something up right here and now! There are distinct differences between fairies and angels: Fairies dwell in the Earth realm in a parallel dimension – Fairyland, if you like – whereas angels are celestial, non-denominational, benevolent beings who are associated with the heavenly or higher realms.

During meditation one day, I asked the fairies, 'How do you prefer your name to be spelt?' They replied almost immediately, saying, 'We care not for your human spellings. All we care for is your intent.'

Well, that told me! Now, I usually use the spellings 'fairy' (or 'fairies'), as most people know what I mean by this. As the fairies told me, though, it is our intent that matters most. Fairies are able to 'scan' our energy and this tells them right away whether we are friend or foe, and what our true intentions are. You cannot fool a fairy, so be mindful of this when attempting to connect.

Throughout this book, I mention a few different types of fairies. What follows is a brief description of some of these. A point to note is that fairies are often referred to using the umbrella term 'elementals'. As this name suggests, fairies are associated with the four elements: earth, air, fire and water.

* Gnomes are firmly rooted in the element of earth, as are dryads, who are the spirits of the trees (although they also have a connection to the element of air, as the trees reach high into the sky). Devas, Pillywiggins and Knockers also fit into the earth element category.

* Elves are also connected with the element of earth, although my personal belief is that they are more akin to unicorns, with the ability to bridge all of the elements.

* Sylphs are nature spirits – fairies of the air. They have the ability to carry our wishes, hopes and dreams into the higher realms.

* Salamanders are fire spirit beings who are present within every flame.

* Water fairies include undines, naiads and water nymphs. I also mention mer-fairies, who are hybrid elementals of fairies (earth spirits) and mermaids (water spirits).

* Unicorns are multi-elemental beings, most commonly depicted as earth and air elementals.

* Brownies are connected with the element of earth, and can be found in human homes as well as in barns with farm animals.

* Leprechauns, too, are of the element of earth. They originate from Ireland but can, on rare occasions, be found in other countries.

This is by no means a comprehensive list of the many and varied types of fairy beings and nature, earth and water spirits. These are simply some of the fairies I refer to within the pages of this book.

Some important things to remember

Fairies cannot be controlled or used to fulfil our whims. We must always treat them with respect, and honour them by honouring the Earth. Fairies are not to be worshipped, but simply loved. Connect with them as you would with a friend, with a sprinkling of fairy dust and cheekiness thrown in for good measure!

Always ask permission before entering any sacred space. I use the following analogy to explain why this is important: Imagine if someone just walked into your home in the middle of the night – or indeed at any time of the day. It is likely that you would not be too happy about it! Asking permission is the equivalent of knocking on the door or ringing the doorbell. A fairy's sacred space is their home. If you wish to gain entry, then simply ask, in your mind or out loud, by saying, 'Please may I approach/enter this sacred space?'

When casting fairy rings (circles) as part of the rituals and activities described in this book, I recommend using a clockwise motion. A clockwise motion (also known as sunwise or deasil) is used to attract energy and/or fairies, whereas a counterclockwise motion (also known as widdershins) is used to banish or repel them.

In the spells and meditations, I often suggest saying certain things, usually in the form of a rhyme. These are simply for guidance until you find your fairy-feet and feel confident creating your own. I urge you to make these spells and meditations more meaningful to you by imprinting your own personality and love onto them.

The majority of the exercises, rituals, spells, meditations and incantations described in the book are inclusive, meaning that everyone can participate in them, whether they are able to get outside in nature or not. Fairies are magical beings, which means they can go anywhere they wish!

When venturing outside for one of the magical practices, always ensure you are in a safe space that is familiar to you – ideally your own garden or land, where you will not be disturbed.

Above all, keep an open mind and an open heart, then you're surely ready to start! Be prepared for an interesting journey, full of twists and turns, magic and enchantment.

Preparing to connect with the fairies

While working with fairy energy is fun and exciting, it is also unpredictable, so we need to be mindful of how we conduct ourselves spiritually when dealing with the fairy realm.

This is why it's super important to protect ourselves spiritually before embarking on any communication with the fairies. Fairy energy can make humans feel heady and a little ungrounded. This is because it has a very different vibration to our human energy, which is where the phrases 'airy fairy' and 'away with the fairies' come from. Both phrases imply that a person is not fully here or fully present.

Spiritually protecting ourselves is also imperative because we may inadvertently open ourselves up to other beings and dimensions that are not of our own earthly realm. Sometimes, our light becomes so bright that it can attract other beings, so we need to be very clear about our intentions and make sure that we are using suitable protection techniques. I often liken this to wearing a seat belt in a car, which may sound like a strange analogy! When we get into a car, we automatically put our seat belt on. It is unlikely that we'll need it, but it's there in case we do. The same is true when we use protection techniques. Knowing that this extra protection is in place helps us to relax and gives us extra peace of mind, allowing us to enjoy the metaphorical journey.

Below, I share a few simple techniques for grounding and spiritual protection. You may already have your own protection methods, and that is fine. As long as you do something that makes you feel spiritually *safe*, that's the main objective here.

The 444 Breathing Technique

Throughout this book, I frequently recommend using the 444 Breathing Technique. This is, simply, breathing in for a count of four, holding the breath for a count of four, then exhaling for a count of four. This technique helps you to relax, and prepares you for your fairy work or play.

Grounding techniques

Several different grounding methods are described below.

Tree roots grounding technique

Breathe deeply, inhaling, holding the breath and exhaling three times to get yourself relaxed, using the 444 Breathing Technique (*see above*).

Visualize yourself sitting next to a powerful and ancient oak tree with your bare feet flat on the ground. See the tree's

9

strong, solid roots growing from the soles of your feet, and feel them going deep, deep, down into the earth. Feel your connection to the Earth, this magical planet. Know that there is no separation between you and mother Gaia. Energetically bathe in this beautiful connection, before embarking on your journey to meet the fairies.

Using food for grounding

Have a bite to eat – perhaps a biscuit or a slice of toast, or a piece of fruit such as a banana – and focus on each bite. Consciously chewing or drinking helps to ground the body, which serves in turn to calm and ground the mind. This is super helpful before *and* after your fairy work or play.

Hands to the floor grounding technique

Wherever you may be, place your hands on the floor, and feel your connection to our precious planet. This can be done on the top floor of a high-rise building or on the ground outside. Your hand chakras will connect energetically with the Earth, thereby creating a grounding effect.

Spiritual protection techniques

I have listed a few spiritual protection techniques below. Feel free to use or adapt them so that you feel comfortable as you participate in the magical practices described in this book. Make protecting yourself a habit, just like brushing your teeth.

The golden cloak

Imagine you are wearing a hooded golden cloak made of the finest material. See yourself raising the hood over your head and feel the sense of safety and protection that washes over you as you do this. Then say:

> *As I wear this golden cloak, I am fully protected, only love and light come near, all else is deflected. My protection stays in place while my golden cloak is on, allowing in only harmony and love, all else will be gone. I am strong, I am safe, protected and loved, always, and at all times. So it is and so may it be, for the highest good of thee and me.*

Bring in the energy of your ancestors

Get comfortable as you use the 444 Breathing Technique (*see page 9*), and feel yourself relax. Then invite your ancestors in by saying:

> *By the power of love and the power of light, I call in my ancestors to be with me this night. Walk by my side, in front and behind, above and below, for we are entwined. Spiritually safe, in your love and your care, calling on you, as I know you are there.*

Call in your guardian angel

I know this is a book about connecting with fairies, but I'm going to bring in the angels for this final protection suggestion. In one of the cards in my *Oracle of the Fairies* deck, there is a card called 'Ask for Help', which depicts a fairy reaching up and calling to an angel for help. This is because every living being has a guardian angel, and this includes fairies.

There are different schools of thought about guardian angels. Some say that they will step in whenever we need them; others say that we have to give them permission before they can assist us. I cannot say which, if either, of these statements is true. However, what I *can* say is that calling upon your guardian angel for spiritual protection is a wise thing to do, as it will give you extra peace of mind during your fairy work.

Your guardian angel is assigned to you before birth, and their purpose is to protect you during your earthly life. Although many religions have stories of angels, they are nondenominational beings, so can appear to anyone, whether they are religious or not.

If you feel drawn to work with your guardian angel for spiritual protection, say the following:

> *I call upon you, my guardian angel. I acknowledge you and wish for you to draw close, to protect me and keep me safe on all levels and in all dimensions and realms. Thank you for your divine protection.*

Archangel Michael is widely known as *the* ultimate angelic protector. Having him by your side is a bit like having close protection security – like celebrities have, but in the spiritual realm. Call upon Archangel Michael as you visualize him wearing full golden body armour and huge white protective wings, saying:

> *Archangel Michael, protector of all, please come to me now and protect me as I navigate the fairy realms. Protect me and keep me spiritually safe, for the highest good of all. I am safe, protected and loved. Thank you.*

Keep a fairy journal

As you work your way through this book, it would be a good idea to document your fairy findings in a journal. Your journal is your own private place to write about your experiences, express your wishes, desires, hopes and dreams, and document any communications with the fairies. It will also act as a record of your fairy journey so that you can look back at how far you've come. More ideas for using your fairy journal can be found on pages 42–43.

How to use this book

You can work your way through this book methodically, from cover to cover. Alternatively, another fun way to use it is to hold the closed book to your heart and ask, in your mind or out loud, to be shown the perfect page and magical practice for your journey. Then randomly open the book and see what appears! I love the spontaneity of the latter method. Remember, though, that there is no right or wrong way to use the book – simply follow your heart.

You'll find audio recordings of the meditations featured in this book in the audiobook version. Listen in the *Empower You Unlimited Audio* app or wherever you get your audiobooks. Listening to the guided meditations will enable you to fully immerse yourself in the visualizations.

Let's begin!

Are you ready to embark on an enchanted journey to Fairyland, where magic and miracles are real and the guardians of nature are ready to communicate with you with open hearts and open arms? If your answer is 'yes', then read on, dear friend. For this journey will be filled with awe and wonder. The 111 magical practices described in these pages will help you to open the fairy door and allow the magic and enchantment of fairies to enter your life, always for the highest good of all.

Create a Fairy Altar

fairy altar is a sacred space for fairy-focus. Create a fairy altar as a special place for your fairy work and play.

Find a space, either indoors or outside, that can be used for the sole purpose of your fairy work. Gather items that represent your desire to connect with the fairies: These could consist of figurines, crystals, rocks, rose petals or petals from other flowers, small plants, incense, feathers, acorns... anything that reminds you of, and makes you feel more connected with, the fairies.

Your fairy altar is personal to you and should contain items that are meaningful to you on your fairy journey. Be creative and remember: There are no rules when it comes to setting up your altar. Think outside the box when adding items to this sacred space. Consider including fairy-inspired artwork, or favourite cards from fairy oracle or tarot decks (*see page 32*), as they are perfect for personalizing your space of fairy-focus.

You may also wish to include items of sentimental value, and perhaps a sprinkling of fairy dust (biodegradable glitter). A small gong, bells, tuning chimes (or wind chimes for an outdoor altar) also make magical additions to a sacred altar space. A personalized fairy sigil is also a wonderful item to add (*see page 112*).

Each time you use your altar, it charges the energy of the space. Adding meaningful items – as well as meditating, saying affirmations and incantations, and performing your fairy rituals and spells in this space – will build this energy in a cumulative way.

Tree Meditation

here there are trees, there are fairies, so this is a wonderful place to begin your fairy journey. This meditation will open the fairy door from your world into the fairy realm, and could be the starting point for a beautiful fairy friendship. It's important to have an open heart and an open mind when embarking upon this magical exercise.

Visit your local wooded space or a garden with at least one tree. Find somewhere within it where you feel comfortable and relaxed, and tune in to the trees. This can be done with your eyes open or closed. Simply allow your intuition to guide you to a particular tree – perhaps the colours in one tree will attract your attention. Utilize all of your senses to find a tree that calls to you instinctively. Ask the tree for its permission to come closer. Usually, you will 'feel' a yes or no energy. The answer can be subtle, so bring extra awareness to this.

Most trees love human connection and will welcome you with open branches!

Next, either sit or stand with your back against the tree's trunk, and say, either out loud or in your mind:

Fairies, fairies, come to me, as I sit (or stand) beneath this tree, for I long to connect with thee. So it is, and so may it be.

Then continue sitting or standing quietly and observe your surroundings. Notice any thoughts, ideas or feelings that may crop up. Pay particular attention to any unusual activity from insects or animals, or to any leaves or feathers that are falling in an unusual way – this could be an indication of fairy activity, and a clear sign that the fairies are ready to connect with you. I would suggest spending at least 10 to 30 minutes tuning in.

Three Wishes Ritual

ost of us are familiar with tales of fairies granting three wishes. Three wishes are also commonly associated with genies, or djinns – supposedly, after granting three wishes, genies are freed from their imprisonment in a brass or golden lamp or a magical bottle.

Try this simple wishing exercise. To add an extra helping of fairy fun, you could imagine your wishes being granted by your own personal fairy godmother, who's just flown in direct from Fairyland!

First, get yourself comfortable and use the 444 Breathing Technique (*see page 9*). This will help you to relax. You could also use one of the grounding techniques (*see pages 9–10*).

Imagine a magical fairy godmother standing in front of you, dressed in a golden, gossamer gown. She asks you to make three wishes, so naturally you oblige. Your wishes should always be for the highest good of all beings and should never interfere with the free will of another.

Now think of your first wish – something that is very precious and dear to your heart. As you think about this wish, hold your hands over your heart and breathe life and energy into it. Then offer it either telepathically or verbally to your fairy godmother.

As you share your wish, feel it with every ounce of your being, and deep in your soul. Smile, knowing that your wish will be fulfilled with the magical assistance of your fairy godmother.

Repeat this two more times, so you have made a total of three wishes. After you have made your third and final wish, say:

> *Dearest fairy godmother, please grant me these wishes*
> *three. I ask for the highest good of thee and me. So it is,*
> *and so may it be. It is done, it is done, it is done.*

Now it's time to leave your wishes in the tender care of your fairy godmother, knowing that we don't always get exactly what we 'want', but we do always get exactly what we need! It's important to fully release and let go of your wishes in love and trust. If there's anything you can do, on a practical level, to manifest your own wishes, then do so – you'll be in harmonious co-creation with the fairies. Listen out and be open to fae inspiration at any time of the day or night.

Make a Vision Board

A vision board is like a map showing the direction you'd like your life to take. The visuals it contains represent your wishes, hopes and dreams. In this instance, you'll be creating visuals to help you manifest a fairy connection.

Find images that represent your desire to connect with fairies. You could cut images from old magazines or newspapers, or search online for words, images, symbols and slogans that are meaningful to you. You could also create your vision board using pencils, pens, crayons or paints. It does not have to be an actual board – it could be in a scrapbook, on paper, on canvas or even on your computer screen. If you do design your vision board on your computer, you could print it to add to your fairy altar (*see page 15*) or to use in one of the many magical practices described in this book. I would suggest placing your vision board somewhere where you will see it every day, as this will reinforce the energy and intent within it and help to accelerate the manifestation process.

The fun thing about creating a vision board is that there are no rules, except to have fun and be creative. Find images that remind you of fairies – these could be actual images of fairies, or pictures of fairy wings, insect wings, trees, plants, flowers and other things from the natural world. You could also include your fairy sigil (*see page 112*) for extra fairy magic.

As you make your vision board, really focus on your connection with the fairies. What does that look like and feel like for you? Bring this energy into the creative process.

It's a good idea to frame your vision board with the words, 'I wish for this or something better, for the highest good of all, so may it be.' This will set a clear intention for what you are energetically welcoming in, while leaving lots of room for the universe and the fairies to fill in the gaps, in more ways than you might currently be able to imagine.

I used to create lots of collages when I was younger. I would spend days carefully cutting images from old magazines and newspapers. I'd get a wallpaper pasting table and wallpaper paste, then I would hold the images high above the paper, and allow them to fall down onto it. It felt as though a fairy, or perhaps several fairies, were assisting me with this fun process.

Music and Song

airies are known for dancing in fairy rings to mystical music. Music really can charm the fairies to your door!

Creating your own fairy-inspired sounds using drums, bells, wind chimes, a harp, a flute or natural instruments will be sure to lure the fairy folk. Tuning forks also work wonderfully for this purpose, as their harmonious tones energetically vibrate between the realms.

Harmonious music and song – light, gentle, delicate and ethereal – will create the most magical musical atmosphere. The fairies will just adore it, and they will draw closer to hear more.

Your own voice can also call to the fairies. Have you tried singing? The sound of your voice filled with love and pure intentions can have far-reaching effects, penetrating the veil into Fairyland.

You do not need lyrics – heartfelt sounds from your soul will suffice. Simply meditate to get into the zone, then allow sounds, tones and vocal rhythms to spring forth. Try not to think too much about this process – just allow the sounds to flow. However, if you're feeling especially creative, try singing specific words, or perhaps using poetry or rhymes to enhance your music.

You do not need to be a professional singer to do this, and if you've ever been told you cannot sing, don't believe it! We all have our own unique voice that can be felt and heard by the fairies. They appreciate real, raw and authentic music and song that springs naturally and directly from the heart.

6

Poetry

airies often communicate in rhymes, so allow yourself to play, let the words and sounds flow and see what happens. You could put these rhymes to music for an even more powerful effect (*see page 23*).

I believe that many of us are closet pixie-poets! We've just not given ourselves permission to express it yet, but this is our chance. My advice is, don't overthink it and simply allow the words to flow. When you fully surrender and get out of your own way, you'll find the words will appear as if by magic. Let your heart be open and your words ring true.

Fairies love to play, so it figures that they also love to play with words, putting them together in ways that rhyme. You could recite a poem about how you'd love to connect with fairies. Here's a super-simple example:

Fairies, can you hear my call? This rhyme is intended for you all. If you can hear, then make it clear, that you are close to me. I ask this for the highest good, of one and all, I call unto you, oh fairies dear, large and small.

Whenever I create songs, rhymes or poetry, it feels as though I am channelling my ancestor, the fairy poet and author Walter de la Mare. Don't be concerned if you are not related to a famous poet, though, as many of us are poets and we don't even know it! See it as a fun challenge and you could be pleasantly surprised, in a beautiful way.

Always speak from your heart, and voice your truth and heartfelt passion for a true connection with the fairies.

Seven-Pointed Fairy (or Elven) Star

Fairy or Elven Star, also known as a septagram or heptagram, is a powerful portal for connecting with the fairy realm.

Those who are knowledgeable about esoteric teachings will probably already be familiar with the seven-pointed Fairy Star. If you are just starting out, then the Fairy Star is a perfect entry point, and certainly worthy of more research as you embark upon your fairy journey.

The Fairy Star is drawn using a single, continuous line. Each of its seven points has a meaning, which can differ depending upon which spiritual tradition you are working with. The points can represent the different directions: north, west, south, east, above, below and within. They can also represent the Fairy Cities (*see page 194*): Gorias (east), Finias (south), Murias (west), Falias (north), the Centre (Crystal City) and above and below.

The Fairy Star serves as a tool for spiritual protection when used in meditations, pathworking (*see page 160*), spells and rituals. It is also a gateway between the human realm and the fairy realm.

The seven-pointed star is also the geometric shape associated with the sphere of Netzach on the Tree of Life, a diagram used in Qabalah, a mystical system with its origins in Judaism. The tree is integral to the Western Mystery Tradition, and one of its most potent symbols. Netzach is the seventh sphere upon the Tree of Life and represents feeling, emotion and the natural world. Its colour is green and its image is of a beautiful naked woman: the goddess Venus – the morning and evening star.

You can work with these visualizations to form your own meditation journey using the Fairy Star. Always ground and protect yourself before embarking on this spiritual work (*see pages 9–13*).

Fairy star meditation

Either draw the outline of a seven-pointed Fairy Star, print an image of one from your computer or visualize it in your mind.

Find a space where you will not be disturbed, then sit in a comfortable position with your feet flat on the floor. Do your grounding exercises and use the 444 Breathing Technique (*see pages 9–10*).

Imagine that tree roots are growing from the soles of your feet deep down into the ground. You see a golden cord coming upwards from the Earth. You tie this cord around your waist.

You slowly start to float up, moving with the golden cord. Beneath you, you can see the seven-pointed Fairy Star.

As you float up, you say:

> *Fairies, guide me within this element of air, soaring high in the sky, without a care. Lead me in love and lead me in light, knowing I am safe in the deep of the night.*

A beautiful fairy appears – this is your fairy guide for the duration of this meditation. You look into each other's eyes and there is a feeling of familiarity. You feel extra safe, protected and loved.

You are now floating amongst the stars. You see a golden castle and the door is open. You float towards the castle, holding your fairy guide's hand. As you enter through the door, it feels like another land. Everything is golden and glistening, as if it's been made especially for you.

Your fairy guide says, 'Please, make this your home; whenever you visit, you won't be alone.'

You feel so peaceful, calm and relaxed in the magical castle high above the Earth and you feel as though your spiritual batteries are being recharged.

You feel as though you are sleeping within the meditation – a magical and enchanted sleep, a deep rest that nourishes your mind, body and soul.

The golden cord is still attached to your waist and you feel a gentle tugging. You know it is now time to go. You make your way back through the castle door.

Then you start floating slowly down, down, past the stars and back towards the Earth, floating and falling in the gentlest of ways.

You soon find yourself hovering above the Fairy Star where you first started your journey, and you land gently in the middle.

You glance upwards to see your fairy guide waving farewell. 'Until the next time, as they say. I know we shall meet again another day.'

You can feel yourself back in your body and you carefully untie the golden cord around your waist.

Start to wriggle your fingers and toes and feel your body against the surface where you are sitting. When you feel ready, open your eyes and ground yourself again. Then write about your experiences in your fairy journal.

In future meditations, you can venture to each point of the Fairy Star, and each point will have a different quality. The Fairy Star mediation can feel very powerful, so I'd advise you not to do it more than once a week.

8

Oracle and Tarot Cards

airy oracle and tarot cards are a simple way to connect with fairies. Metaphorically speaking, receiving guidance in a reading is a bit like jump-starting your car! By this I mean that a reading can lift you out of spiritual stagnation and provide a much-needed energetic turbo-start.

There are several oracle and tarot card decks you can choose from, including my own, *Oracle of the Fairies* and *Manifesting with the Fairies*. Both decks were inspired by the fairies and share ways to connect and manifest with them.

Take your chosen deck and sit in front of your fairy altar (*see page 15*) or somewhere else that is quiet and where you feel comfortable. Close your eyes and start to shuffle the cards.

Allow your intuition to guide you and, when you feel ready, stop shuffling and place the deck face down in front of you.

Express your desire to connect and manifest with the fairies by saying:

> *Fairies, join me as I glimpse into the future, with*
> *your guidance and love. Show me what I need to*
> *see, that will help myself and humanity.*

Turn over the top card and read the message, either written on the card or in the guidebook accompanying the deck. Notice what feelings arise in you when you see the words, as these can be very telling and could uncover deeper insights. If it feels right, follow the guidance given on the card or in the guidebook. Let this be your fairy communication guidance step one.

The more you work with oracle or tarot cards, the more freely the messages will flow. Sometimes the cards jump or fly from the deck! If you watch my daily oracle card readings on social media, you will have seen that this often happens to me. I love it as it lets me know that the fairies are near and joining in the fun.

It is often said that there is no power in oracle and tarot cards, and that the power comes from our own natural intuition and psychic abilities. However, I can feel the fairy energy in my decks, so to me it feels like a very powerful and magical partnership!

Remember to keep a note of the cards that come out in your fairy journal. This is a great way to monitor your progress.

©BHawkins

9

Crystals

n theory, all crystals will attract fairies – fairies are guardians of the Earth, and this means that they are also guardians of crystals, rocks and minerals, for these are all elements of the Earth. However, every crystal has a different quality, so particular crystals are more potent when calling in the fairies, as they vibrate on the same energy level. Examples of particularly potent crystals include clear quartz, amethyst, fairy stones, Herkimer diamonds, fool's gold or fairy gold, citrine, peridot and rose quartz, to name but a few.

Fortunately, there are many books available through which you can study crystals and their uses in depth. I also strongly believe that using your own intuition when choosing crystals for fairy connection is important. Trusting your own inner wisdom and your gut instinct is the way of the fae.

A crystal grid is simply an arrangement of stones on a base, usually in a geometric pattern. You could create your own crystal grid base using a piece of cloth or by painting on an art board. As you create your crystal grid base, use colours that appeal to you. Remember to hold in your mind its purpose – to attract fairies.

The next bit is the fun part! Go to your local ethical crystal store and intuitively select the crystals that call to you. This does not need to be an expensive exercise – tumble stones and raw crystals are fairly reasonably priced. Nonetheless, set yourself a budget *before* entering the store! Then allow your intuition to soar as you select your stones and crystals. The qualities of tumble stones and raw crystals are the same, so which you choose to use is down to your personal preference. A combination of both can look pretty when placed upon the grid.

As you lay the crystals on your chosen base, focus your intention on connecting with the fairies, as this will activate your crystal grid and amplify its energy.

Another way to find crystals is to actually dowse for them in the ground. I used to live in a valley in Cornwall where there were pieces of amethyst and quartz literally poking up out of the soil. It was a very magical place, and of course those crystals were imbued with the local fairy energy too.

You may also find crystals and pebbles with crystals inside them on the beach. These crystals naturally attract sea sprites, water fairies, nymphs and other water elementals.

10

Affirmations

n affirmation is a positive phrase in the present tense – a declaration of intent, if you will – that you repeat several (usually three) times in the morning when you wake up, and several times at night, just before you go to sleep. In this way, the affirmation is the first and last thing you hear yourself say every day, and this has a powerful impact. The words go into your subconscious mind, so even if you do not fully believe what you are saying, the effect is the same as if you do. Create this positive habit and you'll soon see the benefits.

When I was younger, I used affirmations and visualized working with Hay House! Now, many moons later, this is my reality. So I can honestly say that affirmations have worked and are still working for me. One of the fairy affirmations I say is, 'Fairies work and play with me every day. I am blessed to have fairies in my life. My work is my play.' This has certainly manifested in my life.

We can work with affirmations to connect with fairies. I have given a few examples below to get you started. These affirmations are general – a kind of one-size-fits-all! Feel free to adapt them or create your own, that are more personal and meaningful to you.

* 'Thank you, fairies, for showing yourselves to me.'

* 'I am grateful for the presence of fairies in my life.'

* 'I am blessed to see fairies in my waking reality.'

* 'Fairies are drawn to me for the highest good of all.'

* 'Fairies are just a thought away. I think of them, then they appear in whatever form is best for them and myself.'

11

Fairy Rings

airy rings are portals to Fairyland. They consist of circles made up of mushrooms, and can be found on grass in woodland, fields and gardens. Fairy rings are naturally occurring, and feel very magical.

There are many tales of folk who entered a fairy ring to dance and celebrate with the fae, only to be reported missing for many years by friends and relatives. This is because time can pass super fast in Fairyland, even though it may feel slow. You might feel as though you've been inside a fairy ring for 10 minutes, when in fact, in human time, 10 years or more may have passed!

Always ask for permission from the fairies before entering a fairy ring. You can do this by thinking or saying out loud the following:

Hear me, fairies of this fairy ring, I wish to hear you dance and sing. I wish to share in the joy you bring. If it's OK, may I come in? If the answer is yes, then let me know. If the answer is no, then a sign please do show.

Once you have asked for permission, be still in silence and be receptive to any new sounds, movements or feelings that may arise. If you have been granted permission to enter the fairy ring, you will feel it in your gut. The fairies can communicate with us in many ways. If they wish to be seen or heard, then they will find a way – after all, they are the magical fae!

If you do not feel comfortable, then do not enter the ring. Only do so if it feels right.

12

Keep a Fairy Journal

Keeping a journal or a diary is a gentle way to communicate with fairies. Putting your heartfelt thoughts onto paper – allowing the words to flow through the filter of your heart, into the pen and onto the page – is such a pure and simple way of expressing your wishes, desires, hopes and dreams.

Prepare your journal or diary by cleansing it. You could use your voice to sing or speak your cleansing intentions onto your journal, or an instrument such as bells, a gong or a hand drum. Alternatively, you could waft your favourite incense around your journal in a clockwise motion. I suggest doing this at the new moon (dark moon) – this is when the moon is between the Earth and the sun, and occurs approximately once every month. This is also the perfect time to set your intentions, hopes and wishes. Of course, you can do it at any time, during the moon phase that feels right for you.

Create a sacred space for writing in your journal by choosing somewhere quiet where you will not be disturbed. To set the scene, you could light a candle or burn some incense or essential oils in an oil burner. If you have already created a fairy altar *(see page 15)*, this would be the perfect sacred space to start your fairy journalling journey.

Next, prepare yourself using grounding and spiritual protection techniques *(see pages 9–13)*, before opening yourself up to writing whatever flows through you. It does not have to make sense, for the fairies can and will feel your intention.

Write about whatever it is you wish to experience with the fairies, whether that be contact, connection, communication or something more specific. Keep it very simple and remember: You can write in your journal or diary as often as you like, so try not to make too many requests in one session. Start with one wish or desire, and imbue your words with love and light, allowing your passion to flow from you through your pen and onto the paper.

As you work your way through this book, it would be a good idea to document your fairy findings in your journal. You will be able to look back at your journey and see what worked best for you.

Automatic Fairy Writing

utomatic fairy writing involves allowing your pen or pencil to move over a piece of paper without being conscious of what you are writing. To do this effectively, there needs to be a high degree of trust and a surrendering of the heart. You also need to move your mind out of the way, as the 'monkey mind' will not be beneficial for this exercise!

First, you'll need to meditate to get yourself into the correct frame of mind. Actually, the objective is to get yourself *out* of your mind so that you can channel the words with minimal interference from your conscious thoughts. Meditation does not need to be a complex practice: Simply get comfortable – either sitting or lying down – close your eyes and allow the internal chatter of your mind to slow down. Sometimes, focusing on something external, such as a guided meditation,

gentle music or the sounds of nature, can really help to place you in a state of peace and relaxation.

Prepare yourself by using grounding and spiritual protection techniques (*see pages 9–13*). Ensure that any devices are switched off, or at least have their volume turned down – you don't want to be disturbed by the pinging of your phone. Take some time to ensure that your space is as peaceful as possible.

Then set your intention, by saying:

> *I ask the fairies to write through me, speak to me through words, signs and symbols onto this paper. Speak to me in a language I will instantly understand, even though it may be totally new to my intellect.*

Pick up your pen or pencil and allow your hand to move freely, creating shapes and words on the paper. It might take a while to get the hang of it.

There is no right or wrong with this activity. When you start out, what you write may make no sense to your rational mind. But remember, it's not meant to! The idea is to keep out of your own way, and let the fairies have their say. If you persevere, your writing's meanings will soon become clear.

Create Your Own Fairy Sculpture

This is a fun exercise involving plenty of creativity, and – if you've never tried anything like it before – a willingness to try something new. You do not need to be technically skilled to create a sculpture. It can be as abstract as you wish. It could even be a simple stone or leaf shape with eyes and maybe a mouth! What you're aiming for is simply a physical representation of a fairy – and, as we know, in Fairyland, anything goes!

Modelling materials are readily available in lots of different colours, or you could use standard clay.

On a practical level, this activity can get messy, so put a sheet down to catch any splashes and wear something loose-fitting and comfortable that is *not* your Sunday best!

Find a suitable space in which you will not be interrupted and in which your creativity can flow freely – ideally in a bright room with a calm vibe, which can easily be created using gentle music or nature sounds. Prepare yourself using grounding techniques (*see pages 9–10*).

Keep in mind that your objective is to connect with the fairies, and channel this into your sculpting. Your sculpture does not have to be perfect – just play with the clay!

When you are ready to begin, you could say:

> *Fairies, I'm here and ready to play. I'm going to*
> *sculpt something for you from this clay!*

Then intuitively sculpt the clay. You do not have to adhere to any rules, so please don't judge your creation. Just create and enjoy the process.

When you feel your sculpture is finished, leave it to dry.

As you have created this sculpture with your very own hands, it will have extra special meaning for you. Place it on your fairy altar (*see page 15*), or somewhere else where you will be able to view it daily, as this will strengthen your connection with the fairies.

15

Flower Fairy Meditation

This is a beautiful and gentle way to connect with the fairies of the flowers and plants. The primary role of these fairies is to watch over the flowers and protect them as they grow. They will very often take on similar characteristics to the flowers they are tending. Flower fairies are light, gentle and joyful beings and a pleasure to behold.

Put on some gentle music to set the scene. Burn some floral incense, or floral essential oil – rose is perfect for this exercise. Prepare yourself using grounding and spiritual protection techniques (*see pages 9–13*). Get into a comfortable position and use the 444 Breathing Technique (*see page 9*).

When you're ready to begin, close your eyes and start to count down from 10 to one. At 10, you are feeling relaxed and happy;

at nine, you are feeling even more relaxed, and so on. Continue in this way until you reach one. This is a kind of self-hypnosis.

Visualize yourself in a beautiful fairy garden. The sun is shining and the birds are singing. You can feel the warmth of the sunshine on your face. You feel safe, protected and relaxed.

It is the height of summer and the flowers are in full bloom. Their fragrance fills the air. It's so light and a delight to smell.

You focus on the flowers. There appears to be some activity amongst them. As you look closer, you see tiny fairies flying from bloom to bloom, assisted by beautiful bumble bees.

They're working away, tending the flowers. It's such a beautiful sight to witness.

You move a little closer to get a better view. Then, one of the fairies starts looking at you!

'I see a human,' the fairy giggles! 'What brings you here, human?'

You reply, 'I come in peace and wish to form a friendship with you. For I love the Earth as much as you do.'

The fairy then smiles and summons the other fairies to come close. They form a fairy circle around you, holding hands, laughing and singing, 'Join us in this fairy ring, hear us dance, and hear us sing, join us now!'

You have been welcomed and accepted by the flower fairies! They look glorious and colourful – their gossamer clothing matches the flowers they are tending perfectly. One of the fairies places a rose petal hat upon your head. You know that you have been accepted by the fairies and it feels good.

The fairies then say, 'We have to work now, and it's time for you to leave. Keep your flower petal hat as a reminder to believe.'

You start to count up from one to 10, open your eyes, and find yourself back where you started.

Use a grounding technique and eat something, then write about your experiences in your fairy journal.

16

Dress Up!

As humans, we are blessed to be able to dress however we wish. Express and celebrate your inner fairy by creating a magical fairy-inspired outfit.

Creating a fairy-inspired outfit needn't be costly. Using preloved clothing, or upcycling clothing you no longer wear, is the perfect place to start.

You do not need to be a seamstress. All you need is a playful approach. Mix and match, adding accessories such as ribbons, bells and bows, for in the fairy world, anything goes!

Floaty fabrics with shimmers or sparkles, or more earthy colours that call to mind an enchanted woodland scene, are perfect. Flower crowns, old bridal gowns… anything goes, from your head to your toes!

As you're creating your outfit, focus on the fairies, and allow their energy to assist you in designing your magical fairy attire.

If you need inspiration, then a simple online search for fairy clothes or fairy images and art will bring up hundreds if not thousands of ideas. Remember to keep your creations unique, just like you.

And where to wear your mystical clothing? Well, you could wear it for your fairy rituals and ceremonies, or to a fairy party, festival or ball. You could even wear it to the supermarket if you wished! However, I would suggest keeping your creations especially for fairy work and play, a bit like ceremonial gowns. They will then become imbued with the magic of your fairy workings.

17

Wear Fairy Wings

earing fairy wings is an expression of love for the guardians of the Earth. It's the ultimate 'nod' to the fairies and a way of celebrating their presence. Wearing fairy wings is also a reminder to us to take ourselves lightly and to always care for the Earth, just like our fairy friends.

I created a YouTube video explaining why I choose to wear fairy wings because so many people were asking me about them. My answer was and still is 'why not?' I see fairy wings as a physical representation of my love and respect for the fairies. Wearing them is, for me, a celebration of these magical guardians of nature, and I believe that fairies love to see humans wearing fairy wings too! I don't wear them all the time, as that would be impractical! Imagine going to the supermarket wearing fairy wings. Things could get a bit complicated at the checkout!

I do not feel that cultural appropriation applies in this particular instance. As long as your wings are worn with respect and in the spirit of celebration, the fairies will love to see this open display in their honour. Fairy wings could be worn as part of a fairy-inspired outfit (*see page 52*) or on their own.

You can create your own fairy wings or you can purchase fairy wings from one of the multitude of fairy crafts folk online or in person at a fairy event or market. Some of these wings look very realistic and are a joy to wear.

A super-simple way to make fairy wings is to stretch a pair of women's nylon tights over two wire coat hangers bent into your desired fairy wing shape. You can then decorate the material with fabric paint and glitter to your taste.

Where to wear your fairy wings? You can use your wings as a spiritual accessory, like putting on a ritual robe or cloak. Wearing your wings will serve to enhance the atmosphere of the magical practices in this book. It might not always be practicable to wear them, depending on where you are, but it's certainly worth considering as a part of your magical garb.

Wearing fairy wings in the human realm will certainly attract the fairies, especially if your heart is open and you set your intention for genuine fairy connection. This can be done by believing or knowing, with your entire being, that your light can shine bright and be seen and felt by the fairies.

Attend a
Fairy Festival

airies will draw near at a fairy festival, for it is a celebration of these magical beings. There are now fairy festivals and events all over the world, but if there isn't one in your local area, then perhaps you could create one. That's exactly what I did after the fairies guided me to do so.

A fairy festival is a happy gathering of like-minded and like-hearted people who all share a love for the fairies – whether they believe or not, it matters not!

Whenever people come together to celebrate nature and the fairies, fairies will be present. You can feel the magic in the air – it really is tangible. Imagine hundreds of believers – or 'knowers' as I like to call them – all in one place. It is a marvel to behold and the energy is incredible.

A fairy festival is a chance to escape the mundane, and the challenges of everyday life, for a weekend. It's a chance to experience the joy of fairies.

At my festival, there is music, a full programme of workshops and talks, plant-based food and plenty of opportunities to meet and chat with new friends. There are usually 'fairy ring' opening and closing ceremonies at the start and end of the festival, setting the tone for the start and end of the event. During the closing ceremony, we gather in a circle, hold hands and give our thanks to the land and the fairies for allowing us to celebrate. We also place our hands against the grass and beam love into the ground as a way of thanking the fairies.

Fairy festivals are becoming very popular indeed. If you are interested in attending a fairy festival, you could try the 3 Wishes Fairy Festival. It would be wonderful to welcome you!

If you're wondering what to wear to a fairy festival or event, then why not take some inspiration from pages 52–53 and create your own magical fairy outfit?

19

Plan a Fairy Party or Picnic

Attract and connect with fairies by throwing your own fairy party, or gather together a group of friends for a fairy-themed pixie-picnic!

If you'd like to have a picnic outdoors, choose a sunny day, ideally around midsummer.

Be creative by using natural, nature-inspired decorations and decorative reusable cups and plates – vintage china crockery is perfect for this. When you set out the spaces for your guests, leave an 'empty' space for the fairies. This is their signal to join you.

Bring fairy cakes, of course! You could also bring some local raw honey (although this might attract the local bees too!), some sandwiches and some vegan chocolate for the fairies – ideally organic, but this is not essential.

Fairies absorb the energetic vibration of our food. Once they have done this, you might find that food tastes a bit bland, for they absorb all the sweetness and flavour. Clever things!

If you'd prefer to hold your fairy party indoors, then you'll have more options when it comes to food. Play magical music to entice the fairies, and let the sound of laughter and giggles ring through the air. Leave the windows open for the fairies to enter, if they wish!

You can chat about fairies, and share your fairy experiences with friends. Celebrate your common bond as friends of the fairies. Keep the conversation light and high-vibe. Play fairy-inspired music and dance in a fairy ring by joining hands and moving in a clockwise direction.

20

Liminal Spaces

liminal space is an in-between space – a boundary or threshold between one space and another. Fairies often dwell in these spaces, for they like to peek through the threshold from Fairyland into the human realm. Liminal spaces are therefore a perfect and powerful starting point for fairy connection.

Liminal spaces can be certain places, including sacred sites and stone circles. Such places are portals to other realms, including Fairyland. When you tune into the energy of these places, you can feel a shift in vibration.

However, certain times can be liminal, too. Dusk and dawn are considered to be liminal times of the day. They are energetically *fluid* times, during which other realms can easily cross over into our own, and vice versa.

Liminal times of the year are identified in the Wheel of the Year, which is an annual cycle of eight festivals and celebrations: Summer Solstice (Midsummer), Autumn Equinox, Samhain (also referred to as Halloween), Winter Solstice (Midwinter), Spring Equinox, Imbolc, Lughnasadh and Beltane (May Day).

These are the times of the year when the veils between this realm and other realms are said to be at their thinnest, with Beltane, Summer Solstice (and Midsummer's Eve) and Samhain said to be the most potent when it comes to fairy-spotting. This is the premise of Shakespeare's *A Midsummer Night's Dream*, in which fairies and humans connect and magical and mischievous shenanigans ensue!

Find a liminal place, or choose a liminal time, and set the intention of connecting with a fairy for the highest good of all. Prepare yourself by using grounding and protection techniques (*see pages 9–13*).

Once in the liminal space, or once it is your chosen liminal time, you could say:

> *Here I stand on the threshold, betwixt and between*
> *the realms of fairies and humans. A place where we*
> *can meet, a place where we can greet. Shine your*
> *sparkling lights so my experience is complete.*

Be still and feel any changes in your energy or the energy of your surroundings. Perhaps you'll feel the fairy fizzes (*see page 121*), or you might notice a chill or warmth in the air.

The changes could be subtle or very noticeable. Simply be present and observe these changes, then make a note of them in your fairy journal.

Fairy Bath Ritual

un yourself a fairy bath by adding rose petals, essential oils and bubble bath. Play gentle music and light a few candles to create an enchanted atmosphere. You could surround the bath with crystals, flowers or plants, and, for an extra magical finishing touch, sprinkle in some fairy dust (biodegradable glitter)!

While in the bath, close your eyes and relax. Use the 444 Breathing Technique (*see page 9*).

Then visualize yourself in a fairy stream or lake. The flower fairies and water sprites are bringing various flowers to cover your body. A couple of water fairies are combing your hair. You feel like a fairy princess, as they preen and pamper you in the most gentle and caring way. Feel the nurturing energy and absorb it, knowing you deserve it, as you say:

Fairies, I appreciate and accept the kindness and care you are showing me, helping me to unwind and relax, so may it be.

Then allow your mind to flow where it will. This very relaxing meditation may make you feel like having a little snooze, but don't forget, you're in the bath! If you feel sleepy, get out, dry yourself off and lie down.

When you feel ready, end the meditation by saying:

Fairies, I thank you for nurturing me, I feel your love and protection and return it to thee. So it is, and so may it be.

Then visualize yourself getting out of the fairy stream or lake, and as you do so, get out of the bath (if you haven't already). Pull out the bath plug. Know that as the water flows out of the bath, you will come back fully into your body, feeling wide awake, refreshed and relaxed.

Make sure to ground yourself after your fairy bathing experience (*see pages 9–10*).

22

Fairy Friendship Ritual

To forge a fairy friendship, try this simple ritual. You'll need some gold or silver thread, a jar with a lid, some natural treasures, such as twigs and flower petals (only use twigs and petals that have fallen naturally – never pick them), a white candle and some sweetly scented floral essential oil.

Prepare yourself using grounding and protection methods and the 444 Breathing Technique (*see pages 9–13*).

Pour a couple of drops of the essential oil onto your upturned left palm. Rub the index finger and thumb of your right hand into the oil, ensuring they pick up as much of it as possible. Then take your candle and, from top to bottom, slowly rub the oil into it.

As you do this, say or sing:

As I place this oil onto the candle, I invite friendship as it burns down.
As I place this oil onto the candle, fairies come and dance around.

Next, take your thread and wind it around the twigs and petals. As you do this, say or sing:

As I wind this thread around nature's treasures, I invite a fairy
friendship to manifest, for me, for thee, and for the highest good of all.

Then place the wound bundle of treasures into the jar. Light the candle and carefully allow a few drops of the white wax to drip into the jar. Then place the lid on the jar, saying:

I seal this jar with love and light, with hope and wishes
too. I seal this jar with all things right, for fairy friendship
true. It is done, it is so, may this fairy friendship grow.

Place your jar in a safe space – ideally upon your fairy altar (*see page 15*), or perhaps bury it outside in your garden for a full moon cycle.

23

Holed Stones as Portals to Fairyland

It's said that one can see into the fairy realm through a holed stone, also known as a hag stone or fairy stone. The hole acts as a magical window, enabling you to view spiritual beings, including fairies. In this way, holed stones can be portals to other realms, including Fairyland.

If you are blessed to possess one of these naturally occurring, fairly rare and magical stones, then you could have the gift of fairy sight (*see page 269*). If you peer through the stone under the light of a full moon, or at dusk or dawn, you may glimpse Fairyland.

Know that if you are able to peek through a stone into Fairyland, then the inhabitants of the fairy realm will be able to see you too!

Visit a stony beach and see if you can find a holed stone – or, to be more precise, if a holed stone can find you! Treat it like a fairy treasure hunt. Because these stones are often found on beaches, you could call upon the mermaids and mer-fairies as well as the sea and sand fairies to guide you to a stone, saying:

Fairies of the land, sand and sea, please bring a holed stone
to me. Mermaids, too, please hear my quest, bring me a
stone from your treasure chest. I ask, in all sincerity, please
bring this magic stone to me. So it is, and so may it be.

When you find a holed stone, cleanse it by placing it in the sea or in homemade salt water. You could also waft sage smoke or spray cleansing sage mist over it. Keep it safe until the next full moon, or until dusk or dawn. Then hold it to your eye and allow your gaze to go into a trance-like state. Wait patiently and observe, staying open to any magical happenings.

You could also wear a holed fairy stone as a pendant for protection, luck and good health.

Several years ago, I went through a phase of regularly finding magical holed stones on my local beach in Cornwall. Or perhaps the stones found me....

24

Fairy Feather Spell

The beauty of fairy spells is that you can allow them to arise spontaneously from your heart. Spells formed in this way tend to be the purest and most innocent, and this will win favour with the fairies.

Here is a simple example of a spell for fairy connection.

Look for a small feather. It should be one that has been shed naturally, and which will float easily.

Place the feather over your heart to bond with its energy and to imbue the feather with love.

Hold the feather in front of your mouth and whisper your message to it. You could say something like:

> *Upon this feather, I whisper my wish, from deep in my heart, our friendship to start. Of mutual love, light and respect, here is my wish, dear fairies, may you reflect.*

Then gently blow the feather upwards, allowing the breeze to carry it to the fairies. Trust that the feather will be taken to where it needs to go, and that it will be received by the fae.

Have fun creating your own spells, and always write them down in your fairy journal. Over time, you'll see which spells reap results, and you can allow them to evolve organically as your spiritual journey with the fairies progresses.

Photographing or Filming Fairies

Have you ever taken a photograph, or filmed a video, only to find upon viewing it afterwards that there is an orb or lens flare in it? Fairies often appear as orbs and lens flares in photographs and on film. This is typical of them – always showing up on their own terms! They do like to play.

Now that mobile phones are commonplace, we can instantly take a photo or record a video whenever the mood strikes. Why not make a conscious decision to visit some woodland with the intention of capturing a fairy on film?

Let the local fairy folk know what you are planning to do. They may oblige with a magical appearance, if it takes their fancy. State your intention, saying:

Fairies of this wooded place, please grant me the wish of seeing
your face. A sparkling light, a tiny glow, a magical orb, what
will you show? Bestow unto me this wish with your grace.
So it is, and so may it be, for the highest good of all.

If you take photographs, then you could place them in a special photo album and place it on or near your fairy altar (*see page 15*). You might like to add scrapbook-style elements or stickers, to give the album a vintage feel.

When you view your photos or videos afterwards, be aware of the tiniest unusual details – you never know when and how a fairy might show up!

Make an Offering to the Fairies

It is customary to leave an offering for the fairies. This is a lovely way to say thank you for the hard work they do all year long.

Food and drink is usually welcomed by the fairies. Leave out their favourite special treats: organic chocolate, raw honey, anything natural and sweet – for these are the things they love to eat! Honey mead is known to be a firm fairy favourite.

Whenever possible, offer organic, plant-based food and drink items. Be mindful of animals in the vicinity, as some foodstuffs can be toxic to household pets and wild animals. Fruit is always a winner with the fairies, but grapes are known to be poisonous to dogs, for example. Do some research and always err on the side of caution when leaving food outside.

Crystals, rocks and pebbles are also adored by the fairies. If you find one that calls to you while you are out and about, you could gently move it to a place where you 'feel' the fairies are.

Always be mindful not to disturb any wildlife. Make sure your offering is fully biodegradable and that it doesn't contain any plastics.

When I was a young child, I used to leave rose-water for the fairies, created from fallen rose petals and water, all mushed up in a bowl *(see page 116)*. This was a natural and innocent offering from my heart.

Whatever you choose to leave, the most important thing is your intention – always leave gifts for the fairies from a place of heartfelt purity and love.

27

Write a Letter to the Fairies

airies can be around us without us being aware of their presence. So, when we put pen or pencil to paper, they can see what we are writing. Try writing a letter directly to them.

Your letter could begin something like this:

Dear Fairies,

I wish to connect with you for the highest good of all beings, including you.

Write the reason or reasons you wish to connect with the fairies. Maybe you want to manifest something in your life, or help the Earth, or perhaps you simply adore and believe in fairies and would love a fairy friendship.

When you've finished writing, take your letter and hold it over your heart. Say something like:

> *Fairies, please read my words, written on this paper, from my heart to yours. I wish to form a fairy friendship with you for the highest good of us all. I'm receptive to your inspiration, and request that you please acknowledge that I always have a choice and the free will to say no. I ask this with respect and honouring our mutual love of the land where I now stand. So it is, and so may it be.*

Take the letter and gently kiss it. Then place it somewhere safe – perhaps under your pillow or in a special box of trinkets or treasures. If you feel inclined, you could take the letter outside and bury it in a secret place, known only to you and the fairies.

28

Primroses as a Pathway to the Fae

eloved of the fairies, the primrose, also known as 'the first rose', is also a sign of spring. Find a patch of primroses and there, too, will you find fairies.

Fairies love to dance and sing among the primroses, and if you respect these precious and delicate flowers, the fairies may bless you with love, luck and good health. However, if you trample on the flowers, or pick them without permission, then fairy-favour will not be yours. This is true of all flowers, plants and trees in nature.

To find your pathway to the fae via the primroses, first find a location where primroses grow. They are usually found in wild, wooded places that have not been disturbed by humankind.

Being barefoot is the best way to connect with the fairies of the primroses. However, if you'd prefer to wear socks or shoes, this is permissible too. The most important thing is your intent.

Gently walk to the threshold of the flowers, then stop and say:

Fairies of the primroses, I come here as your friend, an ambassador of the fae, your name I shall defend. Pray, please grant me entry to where the primroses grow, I promise not to harm them, and you I'll come to know. My wish, to see you dancing, upon this primrose land; my wish to meet my fae kin, and join you hand in hand.

Next, stand among the primroses and sense their light and airy energy. Breathe in the love, luck and energy of good health and wealth. Visualize the fairies dancing in your mind. Join them and celebrate with them as you count your many blessings.

Sit or stand in this place and allow yourself to feel the energies there. Then take your fairy journal and document your fairy-findings. Try this at different times of the day, for example at dawn and dusk, and see if you notice any differences in your experiences.

29

Fairy Doors

rees often have fairy doors in their trunks. These are entrances to Fairyland - portals to the realm of the fae. There are specific trees, such as oak, ash and hawthorn, in which fairies tend to dwell. However, every tree is a fairy tree, really, although some trees are more magically potent than others.

Human-made fairy doors can also be portals - powerful portals, in fact! I don't recommend having fairy doors inside your home initially, unless you are ready for all manner of fun and mischief! You might find things going temporarily missing - especially things like jewellery, and other items that sparkle and shine.

Placing a fairy door somewhere outside of your home - ideally in your garden - is an invitation to the fairies. Be mindful of this when you are deciding where to place your fairy door.

The reason I say this is that once a fairy door is open, it can be challenging to close it again, or to lure the fairies back into their own realm!

You could try creating your own fairy door as a craft project. This will imbue it with your own energy and the fairies will feel your essence and intent through it.

Start by finding a suitable 'door-shaped' piece of fallen wood in your local wooded area. Driftwood from the beach also works well. Next, embellish it with tiny pebbles, shells or miniature doorknobs, hinges and so on. Be creative as you manifest your magical fairy door.

You could also paint and varnish it with craft paint, and perhaps add a door number or house name. The possibilities are limitless. Once you have made your door, place it in your chosen place, and say:

> *With my own hands, I have crafted this door, it's*
> *the portal between my land and yours. Enter only if*
> *you come with love in your heart, and merrily stay,*
> *then merrily part. Take no thing with you and bring*
> *no thing in. Let's start our friendship, 'tis time to*
> *begin, I'm happy to meet you, my dear fairy kin.*

This is a very powerful declaration of intent. If the fairies hear and feel you, they will very likely come. Be on the lookout for signs of fairy visitors nearby.

To make the fairies feel even more welcome, you could leave a fairy treat next to the door – perhaps something sweet to eat. Always ensure that any items you leave are natural, fully biodegradable and, ideally, organic. Shiny things and feathers also make perfect offerings.

30

Incantations

An incantation is a next-level affirmation (*see page 38*). It's a full-body, full-feeling declaration into which you add extra energy by using all of your senses. Bring your passion to the incantation and feel it as though it has already manifested.

Using body movement amplifies the incantation by bringing more energy to it. You could dance, jump, bounce, run, walk... or anything else within your physical capabilities. It does not have to be strenuous movement – gentle movement while sitting works just as well. Any sort of movement will serve to fuel the power of your words.

As you move, you could say:

> *I have a friendship with the fairies right*
> *now! For the highest good of all.*

You are making your declaration in the present tense, using your entire body, fuelled by your passion and desire to have a fairy friendship. Always include the words 'for the highest good of all' in your incantation. This keeps the energy high-vibe – you do not want to attract naughty fairies!

Say the incantation using your whole body, making the words into a rhythmic pattern, unifying voice and movement. Say them over and over again, for at least five minutes, several times a day. By doing this, you are fuelling your wish with your full physicality and passion, and imagining it as if it is real right now.

When invoking fairies, it's important to be super clear with your requests, as they can take what we say literally. We must also remember that fairies do as they wish, meaning that they do not always respond to our human requests. Fairies work on their own terms – if they want to do something, they will; if they don't want to... well, they won't! This is far from a conventional connection and it's important to practise pixie-patience.

31

Mirror Gazing

Mirrors and other reflective surfaces – such as still, glassy water, TV screens, metal objects and other shiny things – can be portals into other realms, including Fairyland.

Try taking a mirror into a forest or wooded area, as this can hasten connection with the fairies.

Find a tree and ask for its permission to place the mirror against it. You will 'feel' the tree's answer in your gut – if it feels good, then the answer is yes; if it feels a bit 'off', then the answer is no. If you receive the tree's permission, then place your mirror firmly against its trunk.

Use the 444 Breathing Technique and ground and protect yourself (*see pages 9–13*). Then you are ready to begin.

Look into the mirror and gaze into your own eyes, saying:

I hereby open this portal, for the highest good
of all. I call upon my spiritual and fairy guides
to protect and oversee this practice.

Then continue:

I see me reflected in this mirror against the tree. Tell
me, fairies, do you see me? If you do, feel my heart
so true, reveal yourselves in the way you do.

Continue gazing into the mirror. You may start to notice movement in the reflection, in the greenery. If you are able to put yourself into a trance-like state, you are likely to observe more activity. This is not dissimilar to a meditative state – simply focus on your breath to relax and your mind will naturally calm down.

Stay like this for as long as feels comfortable. Then, when you are finished, ground yourself and, moving your hand in a downwards swiping motion over the mirror, from top to bottom, say clearly and firmly with powerful intent:

I now seal the portal from this world into the other realm.
May any being who has entered this realm now return to their
own. This portal will remain closed until I choose willingly
and freely to open it again. Always for the highest good of
all. So it is and so may it be. This portal is now closed.

If you are not able to do this exercise outside, then you could do it at home. However, I would always advise doing it outdoors initially, until you feel confident opening, and more importantly closing, portals.

Working with portals is not a game, and fairy activity is likely to ensue once a portal is opened. It is therefore essential to be clear with your words and your opening and closing statements of intent.

32

Dew Drops Spell

t is said that by placing fresh dew drops upon your eyelids, fairy sight can be activated. Someone who has the gift of fairy sight is able to see and communicate with fairies easily and naturally (*see page 269*).

This spell involves getting up just before dawn – that magical time when fairies are still active and magic is afoot! Go into your garden, or another place where there are clean and fresh dew drops. Gather the water droplets in the palm of your hand, or perhaps in a special jar or vessel dedicated to your magical practices. Say:

> *As I place this fresh morning dew onto the lids of my eyes,*
> *may it give me clear sight into the realms of fairy. I wish to*
> *perceive the fairy realm, where the fairies dance, sing and*
> *play. I ask this from my heart, 'tis true what I say.*

Then, using clean hands, place the dew drop water onto your index fingers and place these onto the lids of your eyes. Feel the cool dew drops start to warm upon your eyelids. Continue to keep your eyes closed for a few moments until the water has dried. Try not to rub your eyes during this process.

Slowly open your eyes and observe your surroundings. You may feel as though you are viewing a dream. Perhaps you will see fairy lights darting around. As always, keep an open heart and an open mind, and document your observations in your fairy journal.

Only use dew drops from pure places where there are no pesticides – ideally an organic field, woodland or garden. Never place any substance directly into your eyes.

33

Make a Daisy Chain Charm

Many of us have memories of making daisy chains as children. This was something I would do with my grandmother when I was a child, and it is a charming and beautiful pastime.

For this simple ritual you will need some time, some space and some daisies! That's it: The fairies will provide the rest.

Always ask for the daisy fairies' permission to pick daisies. Tune in to your gut and wait until you instinctively feel a 'yes' or 'no' answer. Assuming you get the go-ahead, use your fingers to pick the daisies from the bases of their stems: Do not pull them up by their roots. By picking them in this way you are honouring the plant and allowing the roots to live, and therefore produce more flowers in the future.

Find a sunny spot in a garden or park where there are daisies growing. You could also collect daisies from the roadside, or wherever else they grow naturally. Take a handful home with you, or better still, find a comfortable place outdoors where you can create your daisy chain.

Do one of your grounding exercises and use the 444 Breathing Technique (*see pages 9–10*), then hold the daisies in your hands. You'll need around 20 to 40 daisy stems with their flowers intact for this ritual.

In your mind or out loud, say:

> *Fairies of the daisies, I call you to me now, assist me with this daisy chain to guide me, show me how. How to weave and how to create the magic within this charm, always for the highest good and never causing harm. So it is, and so shall it be, for now and all eternity.*

Now pick up the first daisy and, using your thumbnail, or another nail that is long enough to create a split in the stem, make a small spilt. Repeat this again until all the daisies are prepped.

Take two daisies and poke one stem through the other, pulling gently until the flowers are firmly held together. Continue until all the daisies have been used. As you do this, chant:

> *As I weave these daisies within and without, the magic of this charm will come about. Weaving in love and weaving in light, this charm will make everything turn out right. Thank you, dear fairies, and daisies too, I send my love and blessings to you.*

When you get to the final daisy, make a slit in its stem and pull the first daisy, at the other end of the chain, through it to create a circular chain that you can wear as a bracelet, necklace or daisy crown for extra fairy luck and protection.

You can also place your daisy chain on your fairy altar (*see page 15*), or dry it out in the pages of an old book. The dried petals and stems can be used in your fairy spells or simply sprinkled in your fairy bath (*see page 63*).

Ground yourself and write about your experience in your fairy journal.

34

Be in Nature

imply being outside in nature can open metaphorical fairy doors. Fairies are the guardians of the Earth, so whenever you are outdoors in nature, you can be certain that fairies are not far away.

Go to a natural place that makes you feel relaxed and at peace – somewhere that has an extra special energy about it. Prepare to spend a good amount of time there – perhaps taking a flask of tea and a fairy picnic with you (*see page 58*). Remember to take your fairy journal and a pen to take notes following your experience.

If you'd like to meditate, then do so. If you'd prefer not to, then simply 'be', observing your surroundings and feeling the deep sense of peace that nature brings.

Allow your mind to quiet as you focus on and feel your surroundings. Notice anything out of the ordinary, and invite the fairies to draw near, either silently in your mind or out loud. Recite a poem or rhyme, or use this one if you prefer:

I open my heart, mind, body and soul to nature, home of the fairies, where magic is real. Reveal a precious glimpse into your usually unseen realm. Bestow this unto me. I ask from my heart for the highest good of all. So it is, and so may it be.

Then sit in silence for as long as feels right – this could be for a few minutes or perhaps an hour – and notice anything unusual, such as insects or animals behaving in an unexpected manner or leaves or feathers falling in an unusual way. Finish by using a grounding technique (*see pages 9–10*). Then write about your fairy-findings in your journal.

35

Plant a Fairy Garden

any of us are familiar with the idea of 'fairies at the bottom of the garden'. Sowing seeds or planting flowering plants, shrubs and trees will be sure to attract fairies. Fairies have a natural affinity with nature due to their role as guardians of the Earth.

Ensure that the plants are natural, and ideally not hybrids – unless they are natural hybrids. It is always best to use organic seeds and plants, as their energy will be stronger and purer. In some hybrid varieties, seeds are sterile, which means you have to buy new seeds every year. Natural plants will self-seed, with help from the bees and butterflies.

If you have a large garden space, then you could plant a butterfly bush (buddleia). Do some research and select plants that attract wildlife, then watch your fairy garden not only grow, but thrive!

You could add miniature fairy furniture and little statues or figurines of fairies and gnomes to your garden. Many of these have solar-powered lights, so they can light up your fairy garden at nighttime, making it look even more magical.

Night-scented jasmine and other flowering plants will fill the air with gorgeous fragrance, which will serve to enhance the atmosphere of this magical space even more.

If you have a smaller garden space, or no garden at all, you could create a miniature fairy garden in a planter, terrarium or window box. There's always a way, and – as I always say – where there's a will, there's a fae!

You could place signs with messages such as 'Fairies Welcome Here' in your garden as an extra welcome for the fairies.

36

Create Nature Art

Go into nature – ideally some woodland – and collect natural items for the purpose of creating art. Create this art for art's sake – as your offering and gift for the fairies. They will be observing you, and they will be curious about what it is you are doing.

Only use items that you find upon the ground – do not pick or cut items from bushes or trees.

Place the items in a circle and start to create patterns. Try not to overthink this exercise. Trust your instinct and flow with your intuition as you place leaves, acorns, petals or whatever else you have collected in a beautiful design. You could even write a word or sentence and incorporate it into your design, too.

As you are creating your nature art, say:

*Each pebble, leaf and stone I place, is a calling to the fairies,
please reveal your face. This is my offering from my human
heart, my wish is to befriend you, may this be the start.*

Visualize fairies coming to view your artistic creation. See
them happy and appreciative to see it in this natural space.

If you wish, take a photo of your artwork for your fairy
journal, but leave the natural art in situ for the fairies and
others to enjoy. Ensure there are no large rocks or sticks that
other woodland visitors may inadvertently trip over. Always
be respectful of the local environment and others who
may be enjoying it.

37

Find or Make
a Fairy Wand

Having your own magical fairy wand will allow you to direct your fairy-focus simply by pointing the wand while focusing your intent. Your wand is likely to attract fairies, as they love magical things and activities. Your wand can be a simple twig or stick, or it can be a grand affair with crystals and ribbons embellishing it. It's really down to your personal preference.

Find a fairy wand

While outside in woodland or in a forest, decide in your mind that you are going to find the perfect wand. This can be a wand-sized fallen branch or stick. You can set your intention by saying:

*Seeking magic in this wooded place, in the form of a wand
full of magic and grace. May my wand reveal itself to me, for
the greatest good of humanity. So it is, and so may it be.*

Then simply wander around, allowing your instinct to lead the way, being guided by the friendly fae. Allow your eyes to come into fairy-focus (go into a soft gaze), seeing as the fairies do. As you search, you can say:

*The wood must be free and not attached to a bush or
a tree. As soon as I find my wand on the ground, I will
know in my heart, my wand has been found.*

A magical branch will call to you. You will know it's the right one by the way you feel – you may experience an inner-knowing, possibly accompanied by the fairy fizzes (*see page 121*). Or perhaps you will just feel a hunch.

The perfect time to do this is when the moon is waxing, and/ or just after a storm, when there will be many branches on the ground. The size of the branch does not matter – the most important thing is its energy, and the way in which it finds you.

Do not pick or cut branches from living bushes or trees. Also, be mindful of the fact that some trees are dormant during the winter months, but still very much alive. A little prior research is advised.

Once you have sourced your wooden wand, say thank you, in a way that feels right for you. If you wish to, you could leave a little gift for the woodland fairies. Alternatively, a simple verbal 'thank you' will suffice.

Make a fairy wand

If you would prefer to embellish your wand, to make it more personal to you, you will first need to find a wand-sized stick, twig or branch. Then think about how you'd like to decorate it. You could go for a fancy and ornate approach, or stick with more natural decorations. If you decide you would like a fancy wand, then you could gather some ribbons and sparkling accessories that could be used to adorn it. Get some craft glue and allow your imagination to soar.

For a natural wand, you could use natural items as decorations, and perhaps use twine instead of ribbons. Add anything that makes your wand look and feel extra magical.

Bond with your wand ritual

Take your newly found or created wooden wand and place it upon your fairy altar (*see page 15*). Light a white or neutral-coloured candle to bring light to the space. Burn some incense, or use some sage, lavender or sweetgrass spray to cleanse the area. Play some gentle, fairy-inspired music, if you wish. Create your own unique, magical atmosphere for your fairy work and play.

Next, hold the wand against your heart area and allow the loving energy to flow into it from you. Open fully to your connection with the wood, so that it becomes an extension of your magical self.

State your intention as follows:

> *May love and light permeate this wand, and may all things*
> *good be imbued into the wood. So it is, and so may it be.*

Visualize tiny golden fairies forming a fairy ring around the wand, and a cloud of golden fairy dust surrounding it, too. The wand is coming to life, and is only to be used for the highest good of all. Say 'thank you' to the golden fairies as they dematerialize into a vortex of magical fairy dust.

When not in use, I would suggest wrapping your wand in a dedicated cloth, and placing it on your fairy altar or in another sacred space in your home.

Work with your wand ritual

Now that you have found (or made) and bonded with your wand, it's time to use the wand to work and play with the fae! Your wand acts as a metaphorical key to open the doorway to the fairy realm. Only use it for serious fairy-business! If you have charged it correctly, it will be a powerful tool in your magical fairy-toolbox.

Intention is everything when it comes to connecting with the fairies, and your words must match your actions. Fairies are clever beings, and will catch you out if you are not walking your talk.

Focus your intention and energy into the wand. You could create a fairy ring of energy, using the wand to define the space by drawing an imaginary circle in the air, in a clockwise motion, saying:

> *I form this circle of love and light, to attract fairy beings who*
> *shine so bright. This magical ring draws the fairy folk near,*
> *show yourselves now, make it light, bright and clear. So it is,*
> *and so it may be, I call to the fairies, come now close to me.*

Remember the power of your wand, and each time you use it, its power will grow.

Ground yourself after doing this ritual (*see pages 9–10*).

38

Bluebell Spell

It is said that bluebells have a special connection with fairies. Also known as 'fairy flowers', the 'bells' of bluebells are said to ring to let the fairies know that a gathering or festival will happen soon. It is also said that it does not bode well for a human to hear the bells. However, I believe that if you are fortunate enough to hear the ringing of the bluebells, it is an honour and should be seen – or rather, heard – as a rare and personal invitation to join a fairy gathering.

Let's try a bluebell spell for manifesting your wishes. The spell can also be used in situations in which there is a truth to be revealed.

This spell can be conducted either indoors or outside. It is best to perform the spell in bluebell season, which, in the UK, is around April or May. If there are no bluebells in your area, that's OK, as you can use visualization instead. Find an image of a bluebell wood to familiarize yourself with these magical flowers in advance of performing the spell.

Whether you are indoors or outside, find a comfortable place to sit down. Use the 444 Breathing Technique (*see page 9*) and close your eyes. Visualize yourself sitting in woodland full of bluebells. Imagine the sound of hundreds of tiny bluebell bells tinkling, summoning the fairies to a magical fairy gathering in the woods.

You can see fairies flying in from all directions – a flutter of fairies! They form a circle (fairy ring) around you. They giggle as one of them approaches you and places a garland of bluebells around your neck. This is for protection and is also a truth-telling trick.

If there is anything you wish to know the answer to, ask now, then wait for the answer. The answer may come as an inner knowing, a feeling or a telepathic communication (*see page 243*).

Alternatively, if you wish to use the spell to manifest your wishes, say or sing the following:

> *Bluebells and fairy dells, wishing wells and fairy spells, go to*
> *the place where fairies dwell. Hold a bluebell to your heart,*
> *then make a wish for your dream to start. Make a wish for*
> *the truth to be seen, in the bluebell woods, in a sea of green.*
> *Never to a fairy tell, the origins of this bluebell spell!*

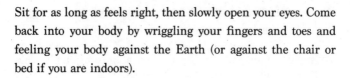

Sit for as long as feels right, then slowly open your eyes. Come back into your body by wriggling your fingers and toes and feeling your body against the Earth (or against the chair or bed if you are indoors).

Straight away, make a note of your experiences in your fairy journal and be prepared for insights and fairy delights to appear in your dreams. Also be prepared for truths to be unearthed.

An important note: All parts of the bluebell plant contain toxins. The flowers should not be picked or brought into the home. It is more respectful to enjoy their glorious colour and scent in the wild.

39

Forest Bathing

In recent years, forest bathing has become popular with people from all walks of life. With its origins in Japanese culture, forest bathing – or *shinrin yoku* – is the art of simply being mindful in a forest, and is known to benefit the immune system and lower blood pressure.

The reason I have chosen to include forest bathing in this book is because of its obvious connection to fairies, who are guardians of the forests as well as everything else in nature. In several other entries, I suggest meditating in nature to connect with the fairy realm. This entry is different – it's about being fully conscious in this environment, keeping our eyes open for signs of fairy activity.

When we become still and slow down, we start to notice more. This works the other way round too, as the fairies can see and feel our energy more easily when we are in a quiet, contemplative state.

For this exercise, it really is best to be outside in a forest environment. Doing this at a quiet time of day when there are fewer people around will enhance your experience. Early morning works really well, and you might have the added bonus of experiencing a beautiful sunrise.

Find somewhere you feel drawn to and sit on the ground. Do your grounding exercises and use the 444 Breathing Technique (*see pages 9–10*).

Focus your gaze on your surroundings, and be fully present in the moment. Be open to any signs of fairy activity.

Notice the green colours of the trees, the sounds of the birds, the way the light moves through the leaves, the shapes the light makes on the forest floor, and so on. The more you consciously attempt to observe, the more things you will notice!

See if you can detect any fairies in the area, for they will certainly be curious about what you are doing, and why your energy has slowed down.

Notice any movements that catch your eye, and follow your hunches if you feel called to turn around and look behind you.

You don't need to ground after this activity because you will already be grounded within the calming forest energy. Write about your experience – including how you felt and anything you saw, heard or experienced – in your fairy journal.

40

Dandelion Wishes

aking a wish on a fluffy dandelion seed head is a beautiful way to connect with fairies. The dandelion is seen by many as a symbol of hope and can be found around the world. Tiny dandelion seeds blowing in the wind represent our deepest wishes. In fact, dandelion seeds – or 'wishes' – gave me the name of my 3 Wishes Fairy Festival! Allow me to explain....

One day, while I was hanging out my washing, I noticed a solitary dandelion seed head on the lawn. My lawn had just been cut (a very rare occurrence!) so this seemed unusual. Suddenly, a dandelion seed 'wish' flew past me. 'Hmm, that's strange,' I thought, as I continued to hang the washing on the line. Then, before I knew it, another 'wish' flew past me! 'This is getting even stranger,' I thought to myself, as it was a clear and sunny day with no wind at all. Then, to my absolute amazement, a third 'wish' flew past me! 'Three wishes!' I exclaimed. It was a light bulb moment. 'Yes, three wishes! That shall be the name of my fairy festival!' I knew the fairies were guiding those seeds past me, and that they wished to inspire me with this magical happening.

The most important lesson here is that we need to be open-hearted and open-minded, and especially receptive to inspiration from nature and from the fairies. This can be quite subtle at times – and at other times, not subtle at all! By slowing down, we can simply observe what is going on around us, with childlike eyes.

Find a dandelion seed head and pick it from the base of its stem: Do not pull it up by its roots. Ask for permission from the plant and its fairy guardian before doing this. Blow the seed head and make your wish with all of your heart. You could wish for fairy friendship, or for a sign that the fairies are near – whatever is in your heart, let that be your wish. Try not to overthink it and let the intelligence of your heart through, as you blow the seeds from the dandelion seed head, saying:

> *Fairies, fairies, as I blow this wish, take it away, to manifest one day. Come what will, come what may, I know this wish will come true someday. Fairies, fairies, hear my call, grant this wish for the highest good of all.*

You could also place some dandelion seed 'wishes' on your fairy altar (*see page 15*), to remind you that magic and fairies are real and that anything is possible when you believe.

Create a Sigil

A sigil is a personalized power symbol consisting of letters and other elements, placed together in an impactful design that can be used to attract and enhance fairy connection and communication. Create your own sigil as a fairy-focus, and a portal to help manifest a connection with the fairies.

Take a piece of paper and, using a pencil, start by writing your full name on it, or a word that best describes whatever you'd like to manifest, then remove any vowels. See if you can create a pattern incorporating the remaining letters. Feel free to flip the letters or turn them upside down, if you wish, to create an aesthetically pleasing symbol.

Add in other words that feel significant to you, such as 'fairy', 'communication', 'connection', and so on. Visualize your desire to connect with the fairies as you create your sigil.

This powerful imagery is personal to you, and is your fairy-connection power symbol. As you create your design, try to emulate the excitement and joy of having a connection with the fairies. Fully feel these emotions, as if they were real. Feelings are powerful tools when it comes to connecting with fairies.

Have fun during the sigil creation process. Allow the pen to flow freely on the paper as you explore different shapes and patterns. As you are doing this, think of a word or a sound to 'charge' or activate your sigil. Then you can use this sound whenever you wish to summon the power of the intention of the sigil. Once your sigil is complete, you can place it on your fairy altar (*see page 15*).

Your sigil has come directly from your higher self. It is personal to you and very powerful. Always use it wisely and set your intentions for the highest good of all, which of course includes the fairies.

Wishing Jar

he beauty of this simple ritual is that you can keep adding wishes to the jar – there is no limit. As and when your wishes come to pass, you can remove them from the jar and either burn or bury them. This is a symbolic gesture of release and a sign of gratitude and trust.

Find an empty jar with a lid and make sure it's clean. Placing a piece of selenite crystal inside the jar will help to energetically purify it. Place the jar on your fairy altar (*see page 15*).

Next, find some pieces of paper and a pen, and start writing down your wishes. You could start with one wish initially. As you write down your wish, visualize it being fulfilled. How will that feel? Allow yourself to feel this deeply while writing your wish and imbue the paper with the energy of manifestation.

Say, 'Thank you, thank you, thank you,' as you fold up the paper and place your wish into the jar.

Continue by saying:

> *As I place my wish into this jar, the fairies come from near and far, to add their manifesting magic here, with joy and laughter and good cheer. May all of my wishes come to be, for the highest good, so may it be.*

43

Make Rose-Water Fairy Perfume

The creation of rose-water – or flower-fairy perfume, as I like to call it – is very close to my heart. It was through creating this magical, fragrant concoction as a child in my grandmother's garden that my own personal fairy journey began. In fact, rose-water popped into my mind as I reached entry 43 of this book, as 43 was the number on my grandmother's front door. Moments like this make the magic of fairies even more real for me.

Making rose-water is such a beautiful way to communicate your love for the fairies. Only use petals that have fallen naturally – ideally from roses that are pesticide-free. Wild, natural roses make the best rose-water.

Take a pestle and mortar, or, if you don't have one of these, a non-metal bowl. Place the petals in the mortar or bowl, collect some rain water (or take some purified spring or mineral water containing no fluoride or other added chemicals) and pour a little onto the petals. Use the pestle or another tool to mush up the petals with the water. As you do this, rose oil will be released into the mixture. Pound the mixture for as long as feels right.

Next, pour the mixture into a suitable container. Then find a place – ideally outside your home, in a garden or in a liminal space (*see page 60*) – to leave the rose-water out overnight.

Place all your loving intentions into the rose-water gift as you say these words:

> *Here is a gift for the fairies from me, it's a token of friendship, I hope you will see. Given with love, direct from my heart, with the wish of a friendship with the fairies to start. I love you as if we are already kin, I am ready now for our friendship to begin.*

Leave the mixture out overnight, then in the morning go and check on it. Whether the container remains full or whether it is empty, know that the fairies will have seen it. Did you know that fairies can absorb the energetic vibration of rose-water? This is why it can appear to evaporate overnight.

Before picking up the container, take a look around and see if you can sense any activity, or any subtle or not-so-subtle signs

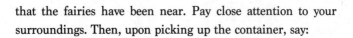

that the fairies have been near. Pay close attention to your surroundings. Then, upon picking up the container, say:

I trust that you have enjoyed this offering from me, a friend of the fae for eternity. Loving the land is just what I'll do, and I send all my love, from my heart to you.

Four-Leaf Clover Ritual

Four-leaf clovers are metaphorical keys to Fairyland. Most people know four-leaf clovers to be lucky, but not many people realize that they can be used to connect with fairies, including Leprechauns.

You'll need a four-leaf clover for this ritual. Ideally, it should be one you found naturally yourself, but it could also be gifted to you by someone you trust, or you may be able to purchase one on the internet. My personal belief is that it is far better to discover your four-leaf clover yourself, as the fairies will often guide you to a clover patch where you will find one, two or even more!

Each of the leaves in a four-leaf clover corresponds to an element (earth, air, fire or water) and a direction (north, east, south or west).

Prepare yourself using grounding and protection exercises and use the 444 Breathing Technique (*see pages 9–13*). Then, as you hold the four-leaf clover to your heart area, say:

> *I hold the key to Fairyland close to my heart. In which element do I start? The earth, the water, the fire or the air? Show me the pathway, and I will stand there. In which direction do I start? The north, the south, the east or the west? Show me the pathway, for me that is best.*

Close your eyes and allow your body to move instinctively in one direction. Don't think about it – just let your body flow there naturally.

At this point, if you have already formed a bond with your fairy guides, they may step forward to assist you. This may happen as a fleeting thought or an inspiration that appears to arise out of the blue. If it feels right, follow it.

The four-leaf clover may also speak to you, emitting its energy into your heart. Be receptive to any unusual forms of communication.

When you have finished, place the four-leaf clover upon your fairy altar (*see page 15*) for a few days, then place it within the pages of your fairy journal to keep it safe.

Feel the
Fairy Fizzes!

Goose bumps, angel bumps or, as I like to call them, the fairy fizzes, are a great indicator that fairies are close by. It's the feeling you get whenever fairies are near. You can literally feel them!

When we wish to connect with fairies we are opening ourselves up to communication with them, in whatever form that may take. Some of us see them, some of us hear them, some of us sense them and some of us feel them. Fairies are creative and magical, and when it comes to the human-fairy relationship, nothing is out of bounds!

Let's try an experiment and see if you can feel the fairy fizzes too! Start by asking the fairies a question. It could simply be:

Fairies, fairies, if you are near, give me a sign,
something so clear. Let it feel like sparkling wine,
your fairy fizzes that make me feel fine!

Try sitting still in silence for a while and see if you feel any sensations. Notice when and how they manifest.

In your fairy journal, jot down what you were thinking and doing when you experienced the fairy fizzes. This will help you recreate the same circumstances, and hopefully experience the fairy fizzes again, in the future.

It is not an exact science, for when working with the fae, one thing you can always be sure of is that they will play!

Leprechaun Luck Meditation

Famous in Irish folklore, the leprechaun is a solitary fairy soul. Leprechauns are associated with the colour green, pots of gold, rainbows, four-leaf clovers and luck. Even though they originate from Ireland, they occasionally appear in other lands. So you do not need to be in Ireland to connect with a leprechaun.

Let's be honest: We could all do with some extra luck in our lives. Well, leprechauns are able to share some of their luck with us, if they wish. During this meditation we will respectfully ask one to do so and see what happens.

Find somewhere comfortable – ideally outside in a natural environment, but inside is fine too, as we are going to use the power of imagination and visualization.

Light a green candle, if you have one, to represent the energy of the leprechaun.

Ground yourself and use the 444 Breathing Technique (*see pages 9–10*).

Close your eyes, and imagine yourself walking in a field of bright green grass. The sun is shining and the air feels fresh with the scent of summer. Suddenly, very light rain starts to fall. It feels cleansing and refreshing on your skin.

You notice a rainbow in the sky, and marvel at its vibrant colours. You follow the curve of the rainbow with your eyes. At the end of the rainbow, in the distance, you can see a tiny figure dressed in green. Then, you see a glimmer of bright light, reflecting off a giant pot of gold!

Slowly, you start to walk towards this magical sight, and you realise that the figure in green is a leprechaun and he is sitting next to the pot of gold at the end of the rainbow. As you draw closer, you ask him, 'May I approach you, with love, joy and peace in my heart?'

It's important to wait for the leprechaun to welcome you. Be patient, as he will energetically scan you first. In less than a minute he smiles and gestures for you to come closer.

You move forward and introduce yourself. You tell him that you would love some of his leprechaun luck, and ask if that would be possible.

He smiles, reaches into his pot full of gold, and says:

> *Take this here golden coin, this will bring you love, luck*
> *and abundance. Always for the highest good of all beings,*
> *including the fairies and leprechauns, of course.*

You receive the golden coin and the blessing of the leprechaun with good grace, and ask if there is anything you can do for him in return. He says:

> *Love and care for the land, and be kind to all*
> *beings, this is my humble, heartfelt request.*

You nod in agreement and bid him farewell for now.

Slowly, come back into your body, wriggle your fingers and your toes, open your eyes and take a long, deep breath. Ground yourself and sit for a few moments as you fully come back into the space and familiarize yourself with your surroundings once again. Then write about your experiences in your fairy journal.

It is important to know that any advice or blessings given in Fairyland are a gift, and it can be offensive to fairy beings to offer any form of payment for them. A gift exchange, however, is perfectly acceptable.

47

Candle Magic

veryone knows that moths are attracted to flames, but did you know that fairies are, too? This means that candle magic is a de*light*ful way to attract the fae! Plus, you don't even need to leave your home.

Find a natural, unscented, plant-based candle. You could use a scented candle, if you wish. However, I find that unscented candles are more potent.

You are going to add your own essential oil to the candle. Ideally, choose an organic oil. Rose is my go-to scent for connecting with the fairies, as this was the flower that opened the metaphorical fairy door for me when I was a young child. However, you can choose whichever fragrance resonates most with you. Something light and floral is a perfect choice.

You may wish to cleanse your candle before you begin, by gently wafting it in burning sage or lavender. Do this while holding your intention of welcoming the fairies. You can easily do this by thinking of your desired outcome – in this case, to connect with the fairies.

Place a couple of drops of the essential oil onto one of your palms. Hold the candle facing outwards from your heart area with the other hand. Then, slowly and intentionally, smear the oil from the tip of the candle towards your heart, saying:

> *As I anoint this candle with the fragrance of rose oil,*
> *I invite the fairies to join me here, with good heart,*
> *happiness and cheer. So it is, and so may it be.*

Next, stand the candle on a flat surface somewhere safe. Take a lighter or a match, and put the flame to the candle's wick, as you say:

> *As this candle burns, may the fairies hear my heart's call.*
> *For the highest good of all. So it is, and so may it be.*

You can substitute these with your own words, if you wish, but always ensure your wishes are for the highest good of all beings.

48

Pick Up a Penny

ow often have you walked past a penny on the ground? Have you ever considered that it could be a gift from the fairies? Well, I can tell you that it is indeed a fairy gift, and it is also a symbol of abundance! Are you ready and willing to receive it?

Some might think, 'It's only a penny. It's not even worth the effort of bending down to pick it up. What can I do with a single penny?'

Whereas others may think, 'Wow! A penny just for me! Thank you, universe, thank you, fairies! For this one penny shall lead to more!'

It's the difference between an attitude of 'glass half empty' or 'glass half full'.

Next time you see a penny on the ground, assume that it's a gift from the fairies, and a metaphorical fairy doorway to abundance. As you reach down to pick it up, say:

> *I pick up this penny, meant for me, and this coin will grow,*
> *so may it be! From pennies to pounds, from pounds to*
> *more, financial abundance now knocks on my door!*

By picking up the penny you are energetically and verbally saying a big YES to the universe and to the fairies! You are showing that you are ready, willing and able to receive the abundant financial blessings of the universe and of the fairies. As the saying goes, find a penny, pick it up, all day long, you'll have good luck!

Place your magical coins in a jar and add the jar to your fairy altar (*see page 15*). These coins can also be used in spells, rituals and for magical purchases.

Invite a Brownie into Your Home

don't usually recommend actively encouraging fairies to enter your home by using fairy doors, because all kinds of fairy shenanigans can ensue! However, a brownie is a benevolent house fairy who actually enjoys helping with the chores! So, in this particular case, I make an exception.

Popular in Scottish folklore, brownies are also known as brùnaidh in Gaelic. They are said to live alongside and harmoniously with humans, and come out at night to spruce up your home.

If you feel as though you need an extra fairy hand to clean your home, then try this brownie invitation. Spring is the ideal time to try it, as it is the season associated with 'spring cleaning' so the vibe is already in the air. Brownies really don't care what time of year it is, though, for cleaning is their love and joy year-round.

Entice a brownie into your home by leaving out gifts, such as milk, honey or chocolate. Your intention must be to offer these as gifts, and not as payment – brownies may be offended by the latter and may never return.

If you need help with a specific task, then try leaving a note next to a gift, stating clearly what you require assistance with. Keep the note simple and to the point, and be polite. A hostile atmosphere will surely frighten any brownies away, so a harmonious tone is another prerequisite for attracting a brownie into your abode.

Placing houseplants around your home will help to attract these house fairies too.

Now, you might be thinking, how can a fairy help me with physical housework? Well, let me explain. Having a resident brownie in your home will inspire you to keep it clean. You might hear a bit of noise during the night – this is simply the brownies doing their jobs.

Working with brownies is not an exact science, and trial and error is part and parcel of requesting their assistance.

Make a note of any house cleaning activity you notice in your fairy journal. Perhaps you will notice that your home feels extra clean and sparkly, or that it has a fresh and clean fragrance.

50

Meet Your Fairy Guide Meditation

At some point during your journey with the fairies, you are likely to connect with a fairy guide. Your fairy guide will protect you and assist you energetically as you spend time in Fairyland. They will also help to keep any unwanted energies at bay.

When they appear, fairy guides often present as fairy royalty – either a king or a queen. They may also present themselves in the form of a leaf-shaped fairy creature, or something totally unexpected.

It can take time for a friendship with a fairy guide to form, so patience is required – or pixie-patience, as I call it! Having said that, meeting your fairy guide can be instantaneous.

You may find that a fairy guide steps in naturally as you make your way through the exercises in this book.

Usually, connecting with a fairy guide will involve testing on both sides – for example, you may scan each other to find out if you're both true to your words, and through this, you will learn to trust each other. This does not always happen, but when it does, it is a beautiful bonus – it's not every day that you earn the trust of the fae. The good news is that there are things you can do to accelerate the process.

'Scanning' a fairy is about opening all your senses and being receptive to any thoughts and feelings that might arise during the fairy encounter. If you have a good feeling, which may include the fairy fizzes (*see page 121*), you know it's a good connection, and vice versa.

What follows is a simple meditation you can use to encourage a connection with your fairy guide.

Find a comfortable place to sit: perhaps on a chair, on a bed or on the ground. Then close your eyes and breathe deeply, using the 444 Breathing Technique (*see page 9*).

Next, visualize yourself walking along a garden path. You can smell beautiful fragrances permeating the warm air. There are birds, butterflies, insects and bees flying around. They are leading you towards a large golden door at the end of the path.

You find yourself in front of the door, and you notice a golden key in the keyhole. You reach out and turn the key, and the

133

door opens easily, as if it has a life of its own. As the door opens, you can see an even more magical path before you – you have arrived in Fairyland! Everything in Fairyland is more vibrant and colourful and you can feel the magic in the air.

You notice fairy lights darting around, flying all about you. They are all different colours, yet one particular light catches your attention. It is larger than the other lights and it is golden. It starts to swirl and spin and transforms into a vortex of golden sparkles, swirling and spiralling until it starts to materialize into a golden fairy queen.

You look in awe at the beauty of this fairy queen. She looks directly into your eyes and you feel enchanted. Her energy and presence is powerful, yet you sense a protectiveness in her too.

She is your fairy guide – your fairy queen. She will protect you as you venture through these magical realms. She may or may not tell you her name: It matters not, for you already know and feel comfortable in her energy.

She points her wand at you and says:

> *My dear human friend, wherever you may wander in these enchanted realms, I shall be there, guarding, guiding and protecting you. For all kinds of beings reside here, and some are a little too playful. As we journey together over the coming days, weeks, months and years, we will come to know each other more. I will be here to greet you when you walk through the golden fairy door.*

You can feel her kindness wash through your soul, in the most beautiful way, and in return you say:

> *My dearest fairy queen, humble and honoured am I, that*
> *you should show yourself and appear by my side. I feel*
> *safe and protected with you as my guide. Speak to me in*
> *whispers and reveal yourself in my dreams, and lead me*
> *through this landscape where nothing is quite as it seems.*

Absorb how this beautiful connection feels for a while. Smile sincerely and nod to the queen, then visualize yourself slowly turning around and making your way back towards the golden door, which is still ajar. Step over the threshold between Fairyland and the human realm and close the door behind you, remembering to turn the golden key to lock it.

Visualize yourself back where you started. Feel your body against the chair, bed or ground, and slowly start to wriggle your fingers and toes, then open your eyes.

Finally, use grounding techniques to ensure you are fully back in the human realm (*see pages 9–10*).

51

Fairies of Light Meditation

everal years ago, I was fortunate enough to meet Brian Froud, a prolific fairy artist known for his contributions, along with his wife Wendy, to films including *The Dark Crystal*, and *Labyrinth* starring David Bowie. Brian also illustrates oracle decks, and in one of those decks, called *The Faerie's Oracle*, he painted fairy beings of geometric patterns and light, called the Singers. I was so enchanted with these healing fairies that I have channelled a meditation through which you can meet them too.

Find a comfortable space in which you will not be interrupted. Ground yourself and use the 444 Breathing Technique (*see page 9*). Do not play any background music for this meditation, as these fairies may wish to sing to you.

Close your eyes and visualize a circle of golden fairies, all holding hands around you, forming a fairy ring of protection. They begin to chant the *Om* sound (the frequency of the universe).

A swirling vortex of golden light appears in the centre of the circle. Slowly, it starts to form into a fairy, with strands of light reaching out to you, as if you're about to receive a healing fairy hug.

You feel the fairy fizzes (*see page 121*) as the strands of fairy light embrace you. You feel safe, protected and loved – held in the beautiful sound vibration of the *Om*.

Then several more formless fairies appear, filled with pure love and light, with an almost angelic vibration. Simultaneously, they begin to ascend as their energy rises upwards towards the heavens.

You then see a vision of our beautiful planet in the centre of the circle, and the fairies direct their love, light and healing energy onto the Earth.

The fairies then turn to you and direct their healing energy towards you. The sound of the *Om* becomes more powerful, and you soak up the beautiful healing vibrations like a sponge, for there is an abundance of healing energy in the universe.

Stay here for as long as feels right. Then, when you are ready, start to feel your body, wriggle your fingers and toes and slowly open your eyes.

This meditation is likely to make you feel a little spaced-out, so it's important to ground yourself afterwards and eat something light. Try not to do any strenuous activities for a few hours. Write about your experiences in your fairy journal.

52

Believing Is Seeing

ach of us has the ability to sense the presence of fairies, and, equally, fairies can sense each of us, including our intentions. When we simply 'know' with all our mind, body and soul that fairies are real, we are more likely to be able to perceive them.

Ideally, this exercise should be done outside, as being in nature is a powerful way of forming a connection with fairies (*see page 93*). However, it can be done indoors, if you prefer, as fairies are not bound by bricks and mortar. They are magical and enchanting shapeshifters who can manifest anywhere they wish.

Take a few moments to settle yourself, breathing deeply and slowly using the 444 Breathing Technique (*see page 9*). This will help you to feel more relaxed and put you in an open state in which perceiving and possibly receiving communication from fairies is more likely.

Say:

> *Fairies, fairies, I know you are there, please show*
> *yourselves, as I wish, will you dare? I don't need to*
> *see you to know you exist, but a glimpse of your light*
> *will not go amiss. I ask you this from deep in my heart,*
> *could this be the time for our friendship to start?*

Now wait, be patient and use all of your senses to perceive the presence of fairies. Notice any subtle or not-so-subtle feelings that arise. Perhaps you'll experience the fairy fizzes (*see page 121*), smell a fragrance in the air, have an unexpected thought pop into your mind, or something else.

Be open to whatever may arise and be sure to document your observations in your fairy journal.

53

Fairy Familiars

ou've probably heard of witches' familiars, but have you ever heard of, or even considered, fairy familiars?

Fairies can shapeshift into anything – after all, they are magical beings. This means that animals can occasionally be fairies in disguise. I know this might seem far-fetched, but as I said in the Introduction to this book, please do keep an open mind.

When you think about it, it makes total sense. After all, fairies are guardians of the land, and animals inhabit the land, so there's already an inherent connection and a natural alliance between animals and fairies.

Have you ever seen an animal, bird or insect behaving in an unusual way? If so, it could have been a fairy messenger.

There have been several occasions on which I have witnessed unusual activity from an animal and had a strong feeling it was a fairy familiar. A crow left me a red ribbon one day, and it felt very magical and fairy-like to me.

When you are next outside in nature, be on the lookout for any such unusual behaviour. This does not necessarily mean that *all* animals are fairies in disguise, but the ones that are will make it very apparent to you through their curious activities!

Fairies that have shapeshifted into animals have a magical aura about them. Spotting this is pure instinct, and you will feel it in your gut.

If you are a guardian to a fur baby or other animal, they will also be highly likely to see or perceive fairies. If you ever see a cat or dog suddenly look around a room, when as far as you can see there's nothing there, this can be an indication of fairy or ghostly activity.

Of course, we should always be kind to all animals, whether they are hosting a fairy or not! However, this is a fun possibility to explore – and who knows, you could end up with your own fairy familiar!

54

Visit a Fairy Hill

fairy hill is a place where fairies are said to reside. There are many fairy hills around the world, where the presence of fairies can be felt tangibly, especially by those with a psychic or spiritually sensitive disposition.

Visiting one of these places can enhance your ability to identify and feel fairy energy, thus helping you to forge a stronger connection with the fairies. There will usually be a hawthorn tree – one of the fairy trees (*see page 174*) – on a fairy hill, but not always.

Some well-known fairy hills in the UK include:

* Doon Hill at Aberfoyle in Perthshire, Scotland. This is the location of the Reverend Robert Kirk's famous disappearance into the fairy realms (*see pages 149–150*).

* Glastonbury Tor in Somerset, England, said to be the home of the Fairy King (*see page 260*).

* Sìth Mòr ('large fairy hill'), adjacent to the River Findhorn in Strathdearn, Scotland.

* Fairy Glen on the Isle of Skye, Scotland.

* Elva Hill in Cockermouth, Cumbria, England. The nearby Elva Plain Stone Circle is another notable place of fairy activity.

By doing some simple online research, you can probably find a fairy hill near where you live.

Spend some time on the fairy hill, and take a fairy offering with you (*see page 73*). Sit in quiet meditation as you familiarize yourself with your surroundings. Often, there is a magical or eerie atmosphere. You might find visual evidence of fairies nearby, such as fairy rings (circular formations of mushrooms – *see page 40*).

Remember to document any findings in your fairy journal. Also remember to ground yourself afterwards (*see pages 9-10*).

55

Astral Travel to Meet the Fairies

I love this technique, because anyone can try it, anywhere. You may already be familiar with astral projection, which is an intentional out-of-body experience, and lucid dreaming, which is a conscious awareness that you are dreaming. If you are, this technique will be super easy for you. If you aren't, that's totally fine, as I will give a few tips here on how to attempt this unusual form of fairy communication.

This technique is best done in the evening, before you go to sleep. Be sure to keep your fairy journal next to your bed, so you can document your astral fairy experiences.

While you are lying down, do your grounding and protection exercises (*see pages 9–13*) to keep you spiritually safe during your dream-time escapades.

Close your eyes and gently tap your head on your pillow three times, saying:

> *Fairies of the dream world, I wish to astrally travel to you.*
> *Meet me in my dreams and feel my heart is true. Allow me*
> *entrance to the fairy realm, where I may glance your face,*
> *and help me to navigate safely to this magical place.*

Count backwards slowly from 10. When you get to seven, open your eyes, then tell yourself, 'As I close my eyes again, I will become even more relaxed and sleepy.'

Then close your eyes again and continue counting down from six to one.

You will eventually find yourself on the edge of sleep. At this point, visualize a thick golden rope hanging from the ceiling above your bed. In your mind's eye, reach out to hold the rope, and then let go. Do this three times. The third time, start to slowly pull yourself up the golden rope. Do this with your eyes closed.

You may wish to communicate with one or more fairies. Imagine how this might feel and what it might look like. There's plenty of room for artistic licence with this. Allow your imagination to soar freely.

Next, focus on your desired dream-time destination: Fairyland. Hold an image of Fairyland in your mind, visualizing it as if it is real, and see yourself climbing up the golden rope into the astral realms. Then see yourself flying with the fairies, giggling and having fun, knowing that you are safe, protected and loved at all times.

Allow your astral body to fly free, knowing it will travel to where it needs to be. Enjoy the experience.

The beauty of this method is that you can do it nightly (if you wish). Each time you will get a little more familiar with travelling in the astral realms and your lucid dreaming abilities will become a little more refined.

Fairy Time

ime is a human-made construct. Fairies do not adhere to human timeframes, or human measurements of time – in fact, they care not for them! Fairies live in harmony with the natural cycles, and their 'clocks' are the sunrise and moonrise, the new and full moons, dusk and dawn and the turning of the seasons.

When you work or play with fairies, time takes on an entirely new meaning and feeling! We've all heard stories about humans who wander into Fairyland and then emerge believing they were only there for a few hours, when in fact they'd been there for days, weeks, months or even years!

There are some well-known accounts of this unusual occurrence, including the story of Reverend Robert Kirk, known as the Fairy Minister of Aberfoyle in Scotland, UK. He was the author of *The Secret Commonwealth of Elves, Fauns and Fairies* (1691), which recounts his experiences within the fairy realm. His body was found on Doon Hill in Aberfoyle. It was thought that his soul had been carried away by the fairies, and to this day his death and what actually happened to him in Fairyland remain a mystery.

You can actively place yourself in this time-less space. This is best done either early in the morning, while you are still sleepy, or late at night, when you are feeling tired. Either way, it should ideally be done lying down.

If you have any time-telling devices nearby, be sure to turn them off. The ticktock of a clock will be a constant reminder of human time, and for the purpose of this exercise, your aim is to escape human time, so you can move closer to the fairies.

When you feel ready, allow the sleepy energy to envelope you, as if you're being lured back to sleep, but do your best to stay awake. Sit upright if you need to, and say:

I am residing in this time-less place, where fairies dwell, in this liminal space. The in-between, the unheard and unseen, I know you are there, show yourselves, be aware of the human that's here, calling to you – oh, fairies of love and light, I am true. I've entered your time-less space, now won't you show me your face? Or perhaps a glimmer of light, that penetrates the night, a glimpse of your love, and a glimpse of your light.

Now allow yourself to drift into the time-less space between sleep and wakefulness – the liminal space where the fairies dwell. Afterwards, document your experiences in your fairy journal.

Fairy Invitation Ritual

A ritual is a series of activities that may include speaking, lighting candles, burning incense, moving your body and other symbolic and meaningful gestures. You can enact simple and powerful rituals to invite the fairies into your life and to begin – or enhance – fairy friendship. Creating informal, intuitive rituals will bring you closer to the fairies, and vice versa.

Fairies are simple beings. They speak the truth, albeit often in riddles! They can read your thoughts and see your actions. They love honesty and truthful hearts.

A word to the wise – fairies will probably trip you up if you do not walk your talk! So, be immaculate in your thoughts, deeds and actions.

What follows is a simple fairy invitation ritual that you can try now.

Go to your fairy altar (*see page 15*) and prepare the space by lighting a candle and burning some incense. By doing this, you are letting your subconscious and conscious mind know that a magical practice is about to begin. You are setting the spiritual scene, if you like.

Have some paints, pens or coloured pencils nearby, as well as some paper or canvas.

Start by performing your grounding and protection exercises (*see pages 9–13*). Then use the 444 Breathing Technique (*see page 9*).

When you are ready, place your hands over your heart area, and say:

> *Fairies, hear me calling to you, sincerely and for the greatest good*
> *of all. I wish to connect with you now, please give me a sign of*
> *when and how. Inspire and whisper to me in my dreams, send*
> *me magic on glistening moonbeams. Tickle my nose at the start*
> *of the day, please, let me see you, and together we'll play!*

Be silent and observe the energy. Has it changed? Take a pen, or perhaps colouring pencils or paints, and allow your creativity to flow freely. Try – or rather *don't* try – to simply allow the colours to flow onto the paper. Whatever you create now is a representation of your experience. It might not make sense to anyone else, but it will make sense to you, on a deep level. I suggest keeping your creation for your eyes only, as it is a magical, artistic manifestation of your inner spiritual world.

Remain open-hearted and open-minded in any dealings with the fae. There is not much room for the rational mind when interacting with the fairy realm. Questions and analysis can get in the way of your connection with fairies. Instead, allow your mind to flow through the filter of your heart. This is a beautiful, natural and intuitive state of being.

After every ritual, meditation or spell, it is essential to close yourself down. To do this, I recommend visualizing the seven chakra points on your body (crown, third eye, throat, heart, solar plexus, sacral and root) as open flowers. Visualize the petals closing as you work your way from top to bottom. Then proceed with grounding yourself.

58

Peter Pan
Incantation

This is a sweet incantation, inspired by Peter Pan's attempt to keep Tinker Bell alive. Along with his friends, he chants passionately, 'I do believe in fairies, I do, I do, I do!'

Peter's passion and love for his fairy friend brings her fully to life, because she feels his desire for her to live. In this way, it's actually a powerful incantation.

We chanted this at my 3 Wishes Fairy Festival a few years ago, and it was a very powerful and magical experience. Everyone – young and old – chanting and singing together raised the vibration tangibly.

Try it for yourself. Ideally, be outside – in nature, in a wild part of a garden or in woodland. Make sure you are free to use your voice in an uninhibited way. Then, when you feel ready, say:

Fairies, fairies, I am here, and I'm about to make my feelings clear.
Let me know if you can hear as I chant this incantation – I do
believe in fairies, I do, I do, I do. I do believe in fairies, I do believe
in YOU! Feel my words of passion, and know them to be true.

Repeat this three times, then sit in silence to perceive any happenings. These may be feelings and sensations, such as the fairy fizzes (*see page 121*), or perhaps a sweet scent in the air, movement in your peripheral vision, fairy lights, or anything else out of the ordinary. Be sure to write about whatever you perceive in your fairy journal.

59

Fairy Lights

I n the Introduction to this book, I wrote about my first experiences of fairies in my grandmother's garden. There, I would see fairies as tiny points of bright and vibrant light, darting here and there in many vivid colours - purple, pink, blue, green, gold and silvery white. These fairy lights pierced through the veil from Fairyland, wanting to give me a glimpse of their sacred forms. Their curiosity brought them close to me, and they have stayed with me ever since, for I have always welcomed and accepted these often misunderstood guardians of nature.

As a comparison, I have also witnessed angel lights. My experience is that angel lights tend to appear in pale shades - light blue, white or gold - and they are much larger and slower than fairy lights.

Fairy lights will often appear to me when someone else is near - usually someone with a fairy vibe. Sometimes, they'll land on a person's throat, and I know that whatever the person is about to say will be significant.

As you familiarize yourself with the patterns and movements of fairy lights, you'll start to know what the different lights and their positioning means to you. This is a beautiful and magical form of fairy communication.

Fairy lights will only appear if and when the fairies want them to – we certainly cannot force them. What we *can* do is put ourselves in a meditative space so that we can perceive fairy lights more easily. Try the following meditation as a potential pathway to perceive fairy lights.

Get into a comfortable position somewhere (either indoors or outside) where you will not be interrupted. Use the 444 Breathing Technique and ground yourself (*see pages 9–10*). When you feel ready, say:

> *Fairies, please show me your light, shining clear and shining*
> *bright, in the darkness of the night, make ready now, to take*
> *flight. As you soar, show off your glow, only you and I need know!*
> *Show me now, please, make it so, and grateful I shall be.*

Be in this space for at least 10 minutes – longer if you can – and be receptive to the appearance of fairy lights. They often appear as a fairy-flash seen out of the corner of your eye.

When you are ready, remember to ground yourself again and write down anything of significance in your fairy journal.

Make a Set of
Fairy Bells

ou may have heard of witches' bells, but have you heard of fairy bells? These tiny bells are hung on entrances and doorways to deter unwanted and uninvited energies, thereby protecting hearth and home. In this magical practice, I'm going to show you how to create your own set of fairy bells.

Before I continue, I know that some will say, 'I thought fairies disliked metal.' My response to this is that some fairies do, and some fairies don't! There are fairy horses, which means that there are fairy blacksmiths – and, of course, gnomes work underground with metals. The origins of fairies' dislike of metal stems from church bells. Historically, fairies were not popular or welcomed within the church, so whenever they heard the bells chime, they would flee.

For this fun crafting exercise you'll need some ribbon, in a colour of your choice, and seven tiny bells. These can be purchased online or from your local craft store. That's it! You can add extra adornments to your bells, if you wish – for example, dried or faux flowers, acorns, keys and other charms.

Take your ribbon and fold it in half, then tie a knot with a small loop at the midway point. This is where you will hang the bells above a doorway when they are completed.

Next, start to thread the bells onto the ribbon, tying tiny knots to create even spaces between each bell. As there are seven bells, there will be three bells on one side and four on the other.

Add your adornments, if desired, and *voilà*! That's it – your fairy bells are now ready to hang.

As you affix them to the doorframe, say:

> *I hang these fairy bells to protect my home from unwanted and uninvited energies. Only fairies of love and light may pass through my doorway. So it is, and so may it be, my home is protected, eternally.*

You can place fairy bells on every door in your home, if you wish. They also make beautiful gifts. Each time you hear the bells ring, you'll know that a fairy is near.

61

Fairy Pathworking

any spiritual practices incorporate pathworking. Pathworking is similar to a guided meditation but with extra elements incorporated into the journey, so that you can easily navigate it. I have created an easy-to-follow pathworking exercise for the specific purpose of connecting with the fairies.

Some time ago, I was invited to a Gardnerian Wicca pathworking ceremony to journey to the element of air. I recall it being such a profound experience and I have never forgotten it. While in the pathworking meditation, I was taken high up into the sky, where I communed with the sylphs, the fairies of the air. I recall feeling that I did not want to leave: I felt so comfortable and at peace in this element. One other thing I remember vividly about the experience is that I felt extremely ungrounded afterwards, as I had not used any grounding techniques. I felt out-of-balance for several days.

If you opt to do any pathworking meditations, then my main advice is to ensure that you are fully protected and grounded before, during and after the experience.

Get yourself into a comfortable sitting position in a safe space where you will not be interrupted. Light a candle and burn some of your favourite incense to create a magical atmosphere. Ground yourself and use the 444 Breathing Technique (*see page 9*).

Close your eyes and visualize yourself standing on a golden path. You can see a golden door at the end of the path. You take 10 steps, and with each step you get closer to the door. With the tenth step, you find yourself standing in front of the door, and you see a large gold key in the keyhole.

You turn the key and the door slowly opens to reveal a beautiful wildflower garden. Nature is abundant here, and there is a deep sense of peace and calm. As you look around, you notice a stream with a small waterfall. You make your way to the water, remove your footwear and step in. The water feels so cool and refreshing. You see several fairy lights flitting around, as if leading you to the waterfall. You sit in front of the waterfall and allow the water to gently wash over you, leaving you feeling cleansed on every level.

A water nymph appears in front of you, smiling. They are holding a large, clear quartz crystal, and they offer it to you. You hold out your hands to receive the crystal and, as it touches your hands, a wave of energy surges through your body.

'This crystal is your gift from the fairy realms,' says the water nymph. 'You can communicate with us by speaking to the crystal.' You thank the water fairy and step out of the stream.

You make your way back to the golden door. The door is still ajar, and you step over the threshold and find yourself, once again, walking along the golden path. You take 10 steps, and find yourself back where you started.

Feel your body against the surface you are sitting on. Roll your shoulders, turn your head from side to side and wriggle your fingers and toes. When you feel ready, open your eyes.

Ground yourself and write about your experiences in your fairy journal.

In the meditation, you were given a fairy crystal of communication, and you can use this to send and receive messages with the fae. You may wish to buy a crystal that looks similar and place it on your fairy altar (*see page 15*) to remind you of this fairy pathworking experience.

62

Feed the Birds

Fairies and birds have an especially close relationship, for they dwell in the same places. Birds are innocent and totally natural, and do not have egos, so their connection with the fairies is peaceful and harmonious. When we show our love for the birds by feeding them, we are displaying our compassion and love for nature, and that will earn us brownie points from the fairies.

I suggest feeding birds natural, pesticide-free bird food and seeds. Larger birds such as crows, ravens, jackdaws and magpies adore peanuts in their shells, as they are fresher that way.

As you feed the birds, the fairies will be watching. Plus, something you may not know (or perhaps you do!) is that fairies can shapeshift into birds and other woodland creatures. A telltale sign that a bird or other animal is actually a shapeshifting fairy is that the bird or animal is behaving in an unusual

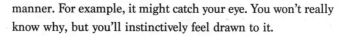

manner. For example, it might catch your eye. You won't really know why, but you'll instinctively feel drawn to it.

Of course, my advice is to be kind to all animals at all times. However, if you do happen to encounter a shapeshifting fairy as you are showing your love to the birds by feeding them, it will certainly win favour with them.

63

Receiving Fairy Gifts

In folklore, there are many tales of fairies bestowing gifts upon humans. Fairies will give gifts as a way of attracting a human's attention or as a symbol of gratitude – perhaps for something a human has done for the environment.

Receiving – or, more importantly, accepting – a gift from the fairies forms a kind of unwritten contract. It's similar to when humans give each other gifts: Sometimes, this can bestow the gifter with 'power' over the recipient. You should only accept a gift from a fairy, or indeed a human, if it feels right and if the intention with which the gift is given feels pure and heartfelt.

Many would say never accept anything from a fairy. However, I would say use discernment, and, as the saying goes, if in doubt, do nowt!

When gifts are given, they come with an intention – an energy – and it's up to you to develop your fairy-senses to see what the intention behind a gift is.

A fairy gift could be a feather, an acorn or something similarly simple and innocent. It could also be something more materially desirable, such as money or fairy gold (*see page 172*). You will instinctively know, by the way it appears, if a gift is from the fae. Perhaps a gift will appear in a very unusual place, for example, or somewhere where you are sure there was nothing before. This is common with gifts from the fairies.

Another well-known saying is there's no such thing as a free lunch! Now, although this is a human saying, there is a degree of truth in it.

Think and feel carefully: What are you prepared to give in exchange? You will find many schools of thought about this, and it is always wise to err on the side of caution. Only accept a gift if you can honestly feel a loving intention from the gift-giver. When we allow our ego-driven desires to take the lead, we run the risk of falling foul of negative intentions.

You could, however, switch the whole thing around, and think, why would fairies accept a gift from me, yet I would not accept one from them? It almost feels rude not to accept! To truly form a fairy friendship, there must be respect and honesty on both sides.

Personally, I feel that if a fairy has graciously gifted you something, it is an honour to accept it. We humans make offerings to the fairies, so why wouldn't they make offerings to us, too? It works both ways.

Although this is what feels right for me, it may not be right for you. Ultimately, it is a personal choice that only you can make.

64

Fairy Food for Thought

t is often said that you should never eat food given to you by a fairy. My personal view is that if you visit a friend's home and they cook you a meal, you would usually accept it, so why should food from fairies be any different? Others might say this is folly! As with other gifts from the fairies (*see page 165*), the most important thing is the intention with which the food is offered.

Fairy food is natural, organic, extra juicy and flavoursome. It is moreish, and leaves you wanting more. Realistically, fairy food is most likely to be offered energetically during a fairy pathworking or meditation. On very rare occasions, fairy food may take the form of human food that tastes extra delicious – perhaps an extra ripe and juicy apple which falls

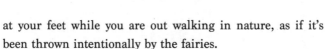

at your feet while you are out walking in nature, as if it's been thrown intentionally by the fairies.

Eating food given to you by the fairies can certainly be a very powerful way to connect with these magical beings – but also one that could potentially have long-lasting consequences. There are no guarantees when working with the fae.

If you'd like to educate yourself further on this topic, I suggest reading the poem *Goblin Market* by Christina Rossetti. It will give you extra insight into the potential consequences of consuming fairy or goblin food.

I would say that it's probably not wise to eat food given to you by a fairy until you are very well-acquainted with each other and have formed a high level of trust after several months – or, ideally, years – of connection and communication.

Ultimately, if you are offered food by the fairies, it is up to you to decide whether or not you wish to consume it. Doing so is always at your own risk, and you must make the decision from an empowered, intuitive and educated position.

65

Bubble Wishing Spell

aking a wish with bubbles is a beautiful thing to do. It not only helps you to reconnect with your inner child (*see page 178*), but also shows the fairies that you love to play!

You'll need some bubble mixture or washing-up liquid – ideally made with naturally derived ingredients – and a child's bubble-blowing wand.

I suggest doing this spell outside, but, if that isn't practical, it can be done inside instead. Just make sure you are next to an open window, so the bubbles can be released.

Prepare yourself by doing grounding and protection exercises and use the 444 Breathing Technique (*see pages 9–13*). Then get into a comfortable position.

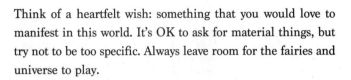

Think of a heartfelt wish: something that you would love to manifest in this world. It's OK to ask for material things, but try not to be too specific. Always leave room for the fairies and universe to play.

Then say:

> *I ask the fairies to carry my wishes away as they rise into the air. Manifest my wishes, with all due care, for the highest good of all, that is not only best for me, but for all of humanity.*

Then blow your bubbles, imbued with your wishes, high up into the sky. Trust and know that wherever they blow, is where they're meant to go.

66

Fairy Gold Spell

ou've probably heard the saying, 'All that glitters is not gold.' It is said to predate William Shakespeare, who wrote, 'All that glisters is not gold.' Whichever wording we use, the meaning is the same: Something may look good on the surface, but may not be all it's cracked up to be.

This brings us to fairy gold, which is a rare and funny thing. It is well-known amongst fairy scholars that fairy gold can, and usually does, turn to dust after the illusion of fairy glamour has faded – a bit like when Cinderella's carriage turns back into a pumpkin after the fairy godmother's spell wears off at midnight.

However, trying to manifest gold with the fairies can be an interesting experiment. Please don't be attached to a particular outcome, though, and be prepared for any financial rewards to disappear as quickly as they appeared! If you're feeling adventurous, then continue....

Start by taking a shiny coin and hold it in the palm of your hand. Say:

> *Fairies, take this coin within my hand and multiply*
> *it to at least a grand! Please don't let it turn to sand,*
> *I will spend it well, and replenish the land.*

In saying this, you have proposed a deal with the fairies, and the fairies pretty much always require something in return. You have promised to replenish the land, so if and when any money manifests, it's important that you keep your word. You could invest in some organic vegetable seeds, plant a tree or two, or something similar that directly benefits the land.

I would advise you not to do this spell too often, as it's wise not to push your luck when attempting to manifest money or gold with the fae.

67

Find a Fairy Tree

airy trees are often found on top of fairy hills (*see page 144*). They can also be found near sacred springs or ancient Celtic chapel sites. Hawthorn, ash and oak trees are well-known fairy trees. However, other trees can and do attract fairies too. As always, with fairies there are no absolute rules, so trust your feelings if you sense that you are near a fairy tree.

In Celtic regions, locals tie 'clooties' (or 'clouties') to the branches of fairy trees. These are small pieces of ribbon, strips of cloth or strands of hair and non-plastic trinkets that are offered as gifts or prayers to the fairies or to the spirit of the place.

Another ancient custom is for people to soak pieces of ribbon or strips of cloth in holy well water before tying them to a fairy tree while saying a healing prayer. As the water evaporates, it is said that any ailment or problem the person has vanishes too.

Visit a fairy tree near where you live and tie a piece of your hair to one of its branches. As you do so, make a wish to connect with the fairies. You can speak or sing your wish out loud, or say it silently in your mind – both methods are equally potent. As always, your intention is what matters most.

Note: There are mixed opinions about the environmental impact of this ancient practice. I strongly advise you only to leave fully biodegradable items. Better still, simply say your wish or prayer in the presence of the tree, then you are leaving no visible trace. On a practical level, the weight of a large number of items is not beneficial to the trees. Be mindful of this if tying a 'clootie' to a fairy tree.

68

Go Fairy-Spotting on Midsummer's Eve

The summer months are when fairies are most active, so it's the time of year when you are most likely to see them! Even though many of us 'know' that fairies exist, sometimes we need a bit of extra proof, and Midsummer's Eve is the perfect time to spot them!

One Midsummer's Eve, a friend and I decided to go fairy-spotting. We ventured to a nearby field as the sun was starting to set. Just as the sun was about to disappear below the horizon, thousands of fairies started flying around! We could hardly believe our eyes! I already knew fairies were real, yet I did not expect to see any that evening, let alone so many of them. We both stood and watched in awe, and agreed that, yes, Midsummer's Eve really is the best time to look for fairies!

Embrace the spirit of adventure and try fairy-spotting on Midsummer's Eve. Wait until dusk, then go out into a (preferably) wild and open space, or some local woodland. Sit quietly in nature and wait to see what happens! Be vigilant and notice any tiny darting lights or other fairy activity. Remain open-minded and open-hearted to what may transpire. Take your fairy journal with you to document your findings.

69

Reconnect with Your Inner Child

airies are often associated with children. Through my studies, I have found that the majority of fairy experiences occur in childhood. My own first fairy experience was as a young child in my grandmother's garden. I believe that this is because children are open-hearted, and their egos are not yet fully developed. The cynical and rational mind that often develops in adulthood is not yet dominant.

Many of us who have early experiences with fairies tend to explain these away with our rational minds as we become older. However, it is possible to get yourself back into that open and innocent space, where magic and fairies are really real! Somehow, I have managed to step out of the fairy closet, retain my childlike openness and fully embrace and love my inner child.

So, a wonderful way to connect with the fae is to reconnect with your own inner child.

Start your days as though you're looking at the world through the eyes of a child. This is a beautiful practice. You will notice everyday things with fresh eyes, and wake up with a spring in your step, ready to embrace the day.

Go outside to play! Dancing, playing, skipping and singing are all childlike ways to attract the fae. Be in nature and celebrate your beautiful life. If nothing else, at least you'll have an extra spring in your step!

Fairies are attracted to the young-at-heart because they possess a purity – a realness – that fairies adore. Try tuning into and releasing your inner child for an entire day, or a week if you can.

Fairy Books

ooks are an integral part of a fairy lifestyle. There are numerous fairy books in publication, including fairy art books, books of fairy folklore and philosophy, fairy tales and books setting out the dos and don'ts of navigating Fairyland. Everything you need to know about fairies can be found in a book, as can some things you'd rather not know! It's all out there, so discernment is to be encouraged when selecting and looking at books about fairies.

Do you have a bookshelf, or bookshelves, filled with fairy books? I know I do! I love flicking through the pages – especially of the fairy art books – as I am immediately transported to Fairyland in my imagination. This, my dear reader, is where it all begins – within our imaginations.

It is likely that you have a favourite fairy book. Think about that book now, and notice how you feel. This is why fairy books are powerful portals into other realms.

Select a fairy book with pictures, and sit silently as you look through its pages, opening your heart and mind to the fairies. Imagine yourself in the art, frolicking with the fairies, leaving behind you a trail of fairy dust and magic. Allow the feelings of enchantment to wash over you, from your head to your toes.

This is a beautiful and innocent way of connecting with the fairies, and the only thing it requires is a fairy book.

If you are feeling creative, you could try making your own fairy book. Crafting is similar to meditation, in that it focuses your attention on one activity, allowing you to enter into a more relaxed state. When we feel relaxed, our minds are more receptive to fairy-inspired ideas.

Make a miniature fairy book

You will need:

* a sheet of paper
* a tea bag, a cup and some boiling water
* a large needle and some thick thread
* a sheet of card
* a quill pen or coloured felt-tip pens
* some scissors

First, take the tea bag and place it into the cup. Pour boiling water over it and put it to one side. Allow the tea bag to brew until the water has cooled a little.

Place the sheet of paper into the sink, on the ground outside or in a paint tray – the sort of large, flat container you put paint in when you are decorating.

Dip your paintbrush in the tea and allow the tea to drip from the brush onto the paper. Then leave the paper to dry. This will give the pages of your book a vintage feel.

Next, take the card and decide what size your book will be – keep in mind that if it's going to be fairy-sized, it's going to be tiny! The card will form the front and back covers for your book. Cut the card to your preferred size then fold it in half down the middle to create the book's spine. Think of a title and write it on the front cover – perhaps adding a decorative pattern around the edges. You could make it extra fancy and magical by using a gold or silver metallic marker pen.

Now take the tea-stained paper to create the book's pages. Cut the paper into sections, depending on the size of your fairy book, and then fold each piece down the middle. Thread your needle and start to sew the pages together along the spine. If the card and paper are extra thick, you might need a thimble for this part.

You could leave the pages of your book blank, or leave it on your fairy altar (*see page 15*) as a real fairy journal for the fairies to write in! Use your imagination as you think of creative things to do with this magical fairy-sized book. The most important thing is to have fun!

71

Live a Fairy Lifestyle

What does living a fairy lifestyle mean? In a nutshell, it's what I have done. As my unique bond with the fairies has grown over the years, their magical energy has permeated pretty much every aspect of my life. My work, my play, my clothing, my reading material – there's not much in my life that the fairies haven't influenced!

Key to living a fairy lifestyle is honouring the Earth and holding a deep respect for the guardians of nature: the fairies. It's about living in harmony with the land, and respecting all beings.

Several years ago, I made the decision to switch to a totally plant-based diet. While this isn't a prerequisite of living a fairy lifestyle, it's something that's important to me personally. Certainly, sourcing organic food is very much in alignment with a fairy lifestyle, as pesticides can be harmful to the insects, which are closely connected with the fairies.

Gratitude for this life, and an eagerness to celebrate this beautiful Earth, also play a huge part. Walking barefoot on the land is a wonderful way to forge an even closer connection with the Earth and with the fairies. Planting fruit, vegetables and flowers – perhaps as part of a fairy garden (*see page 95*) – will also put you in closer contact with the land.

You can demonstrate your love for the fairies in the way in which you choose to decorate your home and in what you choose to wear, making every day a celebration of the fae!

There really are so many ways to live a fairy lifestyle. Below are a few examples of some of the ways in which I live a fairy lifestyle. Perhaps you do some of these things already, too.

★ I attend and host fairy-themed events, including my 3 Wishes Fairy Festival and fairy balls.

★ I wear fairy wings and flower crowns whenever appropriate.

★ I just love flicking through the pages of fairy books and *FAE* magazine.

★ I love watching magical movies about fairies.

★ I have crystals and sparkly things everywhere!

★ My home is a real Aladdin's cave of fairy sculptures and art.

★ I love to express my love of fairies through my clothing by wearing floaty, fairy-style dresses (this style of dress is known as fairycore).

The fairies will certainly notice you if this is your chosen lifestyle. They can detect a fairy believer through their vibrations. So, if you choose to live a fairy lifestyle, you could find the fairies wishing to connect with you, rather than the other way around. How magical is that!

Care for the Environment

airies are the guardians of our beautiful planet. If they see you caring about the Earth as much as they do, they will realize that you already have something in common. This is a sure way of grabbing the attention of the fae, and could be the beginning of a beautiful kinship.

So, how can you show your love for the environment?

★ Pick up litter when you're out and about, or perhaps arrange a beach clean.

★ Choose environmentally friendly items to use in your home that will have little or no harmful impact upon the Earth.

★ Try following a plant-based diet – or start gently by trying 'meat-free Mondays', and build it up from there.

★ Attempt to consume less. Reuse, recycle, upcycle and re-love.

★ Reduce your air miles by choosing other forms of transport, or try a staycation (either stay at home, or have a local holiday) instead of travelling further afield.

★ If you have a garden, leave a section of it to grow wild. Elsewhere, plant organic flowering plants, trees and herbs from seeds that have been produced without the use of chemicals. The more natural they are, the better.

★ Look carefully at how your actions affect the environment and do what you can to reduce your carbon footprint. Walk the walk – don't just talk the talk – and tread gently upon our beautiful planet, having as little impact as possible.

Residing in harmony with your environment is probably one of the most magical practices, and is a great place to begin as you start out on your journey to connect with fairies. The fairies will notice how you treat the Earth, and will be more likely to grace you with their presence.

73

Fairy Key Spell

eople often talk about fairy doors (*see page 79*), but we don't hear much about fairy keys. I wonder why that is. After all, you need a key to open a door. Even a magical fairy door.... The symbolism of a key is overt. Casting a spell involving a key can be a powerful way to connect with the fae.

Try this fairy key spell. Ideally, it should be done at the time of a full moon.

You'll need:

* ★ a key – one that is spare and not currently being used for anything else

* ★ a clean jar with a lid

* ★ dried rose petals

* ★ sage or a similar herb for cleansing

* gentle background music, if you wish, but silence is fine too

Place the jar, key and rose petals on your fairy altar (*see page 15*). Turn the background music on, if you wish. Then do your grounding and protection exercises, followed by the 444 Breathing Technique (*see pages 9–13*).

When you feel relaxed, pick up the key and hold it. Burn some sage (or a similar herb) and waft the smoke around the key, to cleanse the key of any energetic residue. Do the same for the jar and lid.

Next, hold the jar to your heart, and say:

> *This jar is a sacred protected space. Within it I shall place this key,*
> *to show the fairies, whom I wish to see. Upon the key I sprinkle*
> *these petals from the rose. A gift from nature, as everyone knows.*

Place the key in the jar and sprinkle the rose petals on top. Then, as you place the lid on the jar, continue:

> *As I place this lid upon the jar, the key will be activated with*
> *love from afar. I leave this jar out overnight, absorbing the beams*
> *from the full moon's light. This key will open many a door, to*
> *the realm of the fairies, whom I adore. This key is a secret,*
> *bestowed unto me, with provision in place, I shall remain free.*

Of freewill, of mind, body and heart, I rejoice in the knowing,
my journey will start. A journey of enchantment through the
fairies' door, to which I hold the key, how could I ask for more?
And so it is, and so may it be, for I'm the beholder, of this
fairy key, and I know in my heart, they will come to me.

Ground yourself, then take the jar and place it outside, so it can be charged under the light of the full moon.

Fetch your jar the following morning, then wrap it in a cloth, in a colour of your choosing. Put the wrapped jar in a safe place in your home where it will not be tampered with. Leave the lid on the jar for seven weeks, seven days and seven hours.

Seven is the number of points on a fairy star (*see page 27*), which is a powerful portal to the fairy realm. So working with triple seven in this way will mean the energy is amplified – a bit like a fast-track to fairy!

Then remove the key from the jar and place it upon your fairy altar – or you could wear it around your neck as a pendant.

Remember to make a note of the amount of time the jar should be left for in your fairy journal, and set a reminder on your phone if you use one.

74

Sky Divination

ivination is a wonderful way to connect with the fairies. Divination includes working with oracle and tarot cards, runes, flames, clouds, water, stars, crystals, crystal balls, mirrors... in fact, anything that allows you to go into a spiritual space and open a psychic doorway through which information can flow freely between realms.

The beauty of divination is that it allows you to be fully present, so you're able to perceive the past, the present and potential futures. I say *potential* futures because divination shows the flow of energies at play, and so reveals *possible* outcomes, and not final or fixed outcomes. This means that we have the ability to steer our destiny in different directions based on our actions. Having said that, some things are predestined, but certainly not everything.

Divination is a serious spiritual practice and is not to be used for thrill-seeking. We should always be respectful and reverent when working in this way. Only ask questions that you sincerely wish to know the answer to.

Select your chosen method of divination. For the purpose of this entry, let's focus on sky divination. This can be done with clouds or stars, so it can be done during the day or on a clear night.

First, do your grounding and protection exercises (*see pages 9–13*). Next, think of your question, and then hold the idea of connecting with a fairy or fairies in your mind as you focus on the sky. Simply observe what you see. The shapes within clouds lend themselves to interpretation. Clusters of stars, too, form shapes that can sometimes look like words or recognizable images. You might even see a fairy-shaped star cluster or a fairy-shaped cloud!

Visualize your fairy connection clearly in your mind; in doing this, you are sending out a strong signal to your higher self, the fairies and the universe. Sky divination will show you a response to your question. Try to stay impartial (this can be a challenge!) while interpreting your reading. Make notes in your fairy journal. Write everything down, especially the parts that do not make sense.

75

The Fairy Cities Meditations

he fairy cities were briefly mentioned in the Fairy Star entry (*see page 27*). We can access these cities through pathworking meditations (*see page 160*). The fairy cities are Gorias, Finias, Murias and Falias. Each city represents a different element: air, fire, water and earth. They are esoteric realms visited in pathworkings and meditations by those who wish to connect with the fairies of a particular element.

What follows are meditation prompts for journeying to the fairy cities. I have intentionally made them very 'loose' so that you may work with your own intuition, assisted by the fairies and guides for each city.

Before embarking on any of these meditations, always do protection and grounding exercises and use the 444 Breathing Technique (*see pages 9–13*).

Always be respectful of any beings you may encounter in the various cities.

Remember, you have free will and may leave a meditation journey at any time.

Gorias (air)

Stand or sit facing east. Set your intention to enter the fairy city of Gorias. Say:

> *Guides of Gorias, permit me entry to this fairy city of the east,*
> *I ask in love, light and for the highest good of all beings.*

Allow your mind and heart to flow freely, trying not to mould your visions with your mind. Be open to the journey and see where it leads.

Finias (fire)

Stand or sit facing south. Set your intention to enter the fairy city of Finias. Say:

> *Guides of Finias, permit me entry to this fairy city of the south,*
> *I ask in love, light and for the highest good of all beings.*

As before, let your intuition guide you through Finias. Always show respect when entering this fairy realm, and pay close attention to any guides you may meet.

Murias (water)

Stand or sit facing west. Set your intention to enter the fairy city of Murias. Say:

> *Guides of Murias, permit me entry to this fairy city of the west,*
> *I ask in love, light and for the highest good of all beings.*

Flow freely through this mystical terrain as your intuition guides you. Be receptive to any messages you may receive.

Falias (earth)

Stand or sit facing north. Set your intention to enter the fairy city of Falias. Say:

> *Guides of Falias, permit me entry to this fairy city of the north,*
> *I ask in love, light and for the highest good of all beings.*

As you become more familiar with exploring new spiritual realms, let your intuition guide you. Notice any subtle or not-so-subtle visions or messages you may receive in these realms.

After each journey, remember to ground yourself. I also suggest writing about your experiences in your fairy journal immediately afterwards, otherwise the memories may fade. Try to recollect any colours, sights and sounds you experienced, as well as any messages that you recall.

If you wish to explore the fairy cities further, or access more in-depth insights and meditations relating to them, I suggest reading back issues of *FAE* magazine (www.faemagazine.com).

76

Fairies at the Bottom of the Garden Meditation

There are many stories about fairies dwelling at the bottom of the garden, and I believe – or rather *know* – them to be true. I have designed this meditation especially with these garden-dwelling fairies in mind!

If you are blessed to have your own garden, then it would be ideal to do this meditation outside, preferably at the bottom of the garden. If you don't have a garden, then it can just as easily be done indoors, in the comfort of your own home You could sit near a window, so that you can see the greenery outside, or next to a house plant.

Ground and protect yourself before you begin, then get into a comfortable position and use the 444 Breathing Technique (*see pages 9–13*).

When you feel relaxed and ready, tune in to your surroundings. Feel the energy of the garden. Notice how it is breathing, slowly and deeply. Yes, the Earth is alive and breathes energetically.

Close your eyes and visualize a gentle breeze blowing. Some leaves start to blow around you, and on closer inspection, you notice that they have tiny arms and legs: They are leaf fairies!

The leaf fairies are so happy to be in your presence, dancing and singing around you. They form a circle, swirling around you in a clockwise direction, as they start to sing:

We are the fairies at the bottom of the garden, we are the fairies that not many see. We are the fairies at the bottom of the garden, we're so happy and we feel free. We are free to dance and sing, we are free to end or begin, we are free to come close to you, we are free in all we do. We are free from without and within, we are free, we're your fairy kin.

Their jolly song sounds familiar – perhaps you've heard it before. You find yourself yearning for more. The leaf fairies stop swirling and sit with you. You energetically bathe in their sweet, earthy energy. You all meditate together until you hear one of the fairies start to giggle! Fairies cannot be silent or serious for *too* long!

The fairies tell you telepathically that they are happy you came to be with them at the bottom of the garden, and that if you come again, they may take on different shapes and forms, depending on how they feel.

The fairies turn back into 'normal' leaves and blow away. You become conscious of your body, wriggle your fingers and toes and ground yourself. When you feel ready, slowly open your eyes.

Wishing Well Spell

Wishing wells are places of magic and enchantment. You'll usually find lots of coins at the bottom of the well – each one cast in by a person making a wish. The water fairies accept the coin in exchange for granting the wish. It's such a beautiful tradition.

If you don't happen to have a wishing well in your garden or local area, the good news is, we can improvise with this wishing well spell.

You'll need a shiny coin, some fairy dust (biodegradable glitter) and a few drops of clean, pure water – either from a spring or from a bottle of mineral water.

Take a piece of paper and a pen or pencil and draw a circle in a clockwise direction. This circle represents the top of the well. As you draw the circle, recite the following:

Come, water fairies of the wishing well, come close and assist me as I perform this spell. This spell is for the highest good of all, and will harm no being, great or small. I send love and light, to one and all.

Next, think of a wish – something close to your heart. Hold the vision of your wish as you place your shiny coin onto the picture of the well. Drip a few drops of the water onto the well in a clockwise motion, then sprinkle the fairy dust around the outside of the well, also in a clockwise motion.

Visualize the coin falling down, down, deep into the wishing well. See a fairy of the well catch it and hold it to her heart, as she says, 'Know your wish is safe with me, I will manifest for thee.'

Then fold up the paper and place it on your fairy altar (*see page 15*), or somewhere safe and out of sight until the full moon does shine its light.

Ground yourself and write about your experiences in your fairy journal.

The next time there is a full moon, take your paper outside and place it underneath the moonbeams. This will recharge and reactivate the energy of this wishing well spell.

78

Fairy Dust Ritual

his is a beautiful, gentle and very sparkly ritual to attract fairies. After all, what could be more quintessentially fairy than fairy dust? It's time to get your sparkle on!

Get some fairy dust (biodegradable glitter). Put on some relaxing music – ideally, music featuring delicate wind chimes or bells. Then light some incense, and you may wish to light a candle, too.

Start by grounding and protecting yourself, then use the 444 Breathing Technique (*see pages 9–13*).

Ideally, this ritual should be performed standing. When you feel ready and you've created your sacred fairy space, place some fairy dust into the palm of your hand.

Take a pinch of this fairy dust with the other hand, and sprinkle it in a circle around yourself, in a clockwise direction.

If there is any fairy dust remaining in your palm, rub it onto the top of your head. As you do this, say:

I call to the fairies who dwell near this land, I gift magic glitter, in the palm of my hand. The sparkles will carry me into portals true, there we can meet, come to me do. As I spread magic dust within this place, I call to the fairies, please come to this space.

You have made your call: Now you may sit down, close your eyes, meditate and wait.

The sparkles and gentle music will most likely attract some fairy friends. Visualize them coming to you and befriend them telepathically.

Celebrate as though they have already come to you. Then, when you feel ready, ground yourself and open your eyes.

You may prefer to clean up the glitter. However, I would suggest leaving it as a sign that the fairies are welcome. Each time you see it, it will remind you of the ritual.

79

Fairy Hair Ritual

In the fairy world, one can never have enough sparkle! Glitter here, glitter there, even glitter in your hair! Yes, the more glitter you have, the merrier you'll be!

You will need:

* some fairy dust (biodegradable glitter)

* some rose essential oil or rose-water

* some natural shampoo and conditioner

* a brush

This ritual can be combined with the Fairy Bath Ritual (*see page 63*).

Wash your hair with your usual (ideally natural) shampoo and conditioner.

Rinse your hair and towel dry it. Then sprinkle rose essential oil or spray rose-water onto the crown of your head. Brush it through your hair, saying:

> *I brush my hair to imbue love and light into all I do.*
> *May my heart and mind always be true, as I dedicate*
> *my life to you, the Earth, the home of my birth.*

Take a pinch of fairy dust and sprinkle it over the top of your head, saying:

> *May this glitter attract the fae, who, when they find*
> *me, will wish to stay. To brighten my day, to giggle*
> *and laugh, especially when I take a fairy bath!*

For the purpose of this ritual, allow your hair to dry naturally.

You could also tie fairy strands (pieces of metallic thread) to individual strands of hair. I can often be seen with fairy strands in my hair. They are readily available online or at most fairy festivals and events.

80

Fairy Drumming

airies are drawn to rhythmic and natural sounds, so the sound of fairy drumming – especially when done with the intention to call upon the fae – will surely encourage them to come your way.

When I refer to drumming, I do not mean using a drum kit. I'm talking about hand-held drums, of which there are several varieties. You'll need a hand-held drum for this exercise. If you don't have a drum to hand, then you can improvise by using a saucepan, or anything else in your home that you can tap a rhythm on.

Most drums are made using animal skin, but there are vegan, non-skin drums which work just as well. These are the drums I prefer to use.

Everyone can play the drum – you just need to find your own natural rhythm and bang the drum along with it, gently at first, until you find a beat that feels right for you.

As you drum and sing, you'll find that you may go into a bit of a trance-like state. This is fine, as it will help you to reach the fairy realm, where your voice and drum will be heard and sensed by the fairies.

I wrote a song for when I call in the fairies using drumming. It goes like this:

Calling in the fairy energy, drumming in for you, drumming in for me.
Calling in the fairy energy, drumming in for you, drumming in for me.

You are welcome to use my song. However, I encourage you to create your own. Play with melodies and words until your song manifests. Try not to overthink it. Instead, *feel* your way through it.

As you are banging your drum and calling in the fairies, set your intention to draw the fairies to your door. Do this by imagining them flying towards your door as they hear the sound of your drum. You can also visualize your door opening and seeing them flying in, leaving a trail of fairy dust behind them.

Then take a while to ponder what you will ask them for when you meet. Just a fairy meet-and-greet? Or something more? If you've already established a connection with the fairies, then you may have a specific request. If you haven't, then this exercise will be about starting to build your fairy friendship, which can take some time. As always, keep your heart and mind open.

81

Wish Upon a Star Spell

airies come out at nighttime, as well as during the day. Generally, fairies are not confined to either day or night, unless they have specifics tasks to do. Flowers that bloom in the darkness, such as night-scented jasmine, are tended by the night-fairies.

For this spell, you'll need a white, silver or light-coloured candle and a jar. The spell can be done indoors or outside. If you choose to do it outside, then on a night with a full moon and a clear, starry sky would be best, as it will be easier to see what you are doing. If you choose to do it indoors, then you could hold the jar out of a window so that the starlight shines on it.

Find a safe space and do your grounding and protection exercises, followed by the 444 Breathing Technique (*see pages 9-13*). When you feel grounded and ready, say:

I take this candle and this jar, and make my wish upon a star. Fairies, come from near and far, and show me how magical you are. Grant my wish to see you soon, grant my wish, by the stars and the moon.

Then place the candle inside the jar and light the candle. Hold it up high for the fairies to see.

Then focus on a star – any star. Ask the star to amplify your wish to see the fairies, by saying:

Shining star, so near, so far, your magic pours down upon the Earth. Your magical beam, into me stream, to bring my wishes true.

Allow the starlight to enter the jar. When you feel ready, place the lid on the jar and this will extinguish the flame. Then place the jar upon your fairy altar (*see page 15*).

Make a note of your wish in your fairy journal, and follow up on this by recording any fairy experiences you have over the coming days, weeks and months.

82

Meet a Pillywiggin

'What on Earth is a Pillywiggin?' I hear you cry! Well, let me tell you. Pillywiggin is a Welsh word for a flower fairy of the springtime. I love the name Pillywiggin, though I don't usually get caught up in the various names and spellings for different types of fairies as it can be like going down a rabbit hole! The Pillywiggins have a different kind of charm, though, so I make an exception for them. They are generally joyful beings.

Pillywiggins are less active during the winter months, when they are said to hibernate. I cannot confirm whether or not this is true, but I do know that the best time to connect with Pillywiggins is at the start of spring, as they prepare to tend the flowers and new spring growth.

To meet with a Pillywiggin, go outside in the early springtime. Find a location where spring flowers are growing – perhaps in a local park, woodland or in your garden, if you have one.

If this is not possible, you can still participate inside your home – maybe sit close to a window with a view of the greenery outside, or next to a house plant or window box.

Find a comfy place to sit and say:

> *Pillywiggin dance, Pillywiggin sing, Pillywiggin*
> *comes at the break of spring. I will sit and wait*
> *for you, so grateful for everything you do.*

Acknowledging the good work of the Pillywiggins is essential if you wish for them to come close, as they are always super busy in spring. You can assist them by planting spring bulbs and tending them with love in your heart.

You could also create a sign for your garden, patio or window box that says simply: 'Pillywiggins Welcome'. They will greatly appreciate this hospitable message, and it may also entice them to draw near.

83

Tree Roots
Meditation

his is a very grounding meditation, so is very useful if
you are feeling airy-fairy, light-headed or simply away
with the fairies, energetically speaking.

Do your grounding and protection exercises and use the
444 Breathing Technique (*see pages 9–13*). Then visualize
yourself standing in front of an ancient tree with a door in
its trunk.

The door opens and you see a spiral staircase inside. You start
to walk down the stairs, counting as you descend: 10, 9, 8, 7,
6, 5, 4, 3, 2, 1. When you reach the bottom, you can see lots
of gnarly tree roots and a gnome sitting on them. The gnome
greets you with a friendly smile.

'Welcome to my humble abode,' he says.

'Please share your wisdom, that I may take it to my human realm,' you ask.

The gnome replies:

A tree is more powerful than you'll ever know. Trees emit wisdom and have the ability to simply 'be'. Yes, we can learn a lot from a tree. With their head in the clouds and their roots going deep, deep, down into the Earth. They are the most grounded beings I know.

The gnome then invites you to venture even further down, into the Earth, via yet another spiral staircase. You follow him.

After walking down several more steps inside the tree trunk, you stop and see a sea of tree roots. You feel safe, protected and loved in this dark, womb-like space. You gently touch the roots and connect to this powerful force. Feel the energy here – notice how grounded you feel.

The gnome then says that it's time to leave, and you follow him up two flights of wooden spiral stairs. You begin to count when you reach the second flight: 1, 2, 3, 4, 5, 6, 7, 8, 9, 10. Then you find yourself at the top again.

Gently touch the tree to say thank you, before opening your eyes and coming back to your normal waking reality, feeling rooted and fully grounded.

Make a note in your fairy journal about how you felt during this exercise.

84

Manifesting with Gnomes Meditation

In the fairy world, gnomes are known to be the hardest of workers. They are very grounded and can manifest and attract gold. Fairy gold is covered elsewhere in this book (*see page 172*). Gold manifested by gnomes is different, though, as their gold comes from hard work. So, for material manifestations, connecting with the gnomes is a great first port of call.

The beautiful thing about gnomes is that they really do help us to stay grounded, rooted and connected to the Earth. It is from this place that our hopes, wishes and dreams can soar high.

Visualize yourself standing in front of the tree in the Tree Roots Meditation (*see page 214*).

You knock three times on the tree's fairy door, then wait to be invited to enter.

Slowly, the door opens and you are greeted by a smiling gnome wearing a bright-red hat. He has a long, white beard and a cheerful disposition. He gestures for you to enter and points towards a large wooden table by an open fire. There is a pot of tea on the table and a few fairy cakes.

You sit down and the gnome sits opposite you. He pours some tea and offers you a cake. It's up to you whether you wish to accept the cake or not. He will not be offended if you politely refuse it.

He places a piece of paper in front of you, along with a golden quill pen and a pot of invisible ink. He then says, 'Write your wishes here, and let's see what we can do to manifest them.'

You begin to write, but as you do, you notice that the words quickly vanish from the page. The gnome smiles and says, 'As you write, your wishes are being taken to the fairies of the air (the sylphs), who will carry them to the place where dreams are made and where wishes really can come true.'

You continue to write and imbue every word with your love. When you have finished writing, you hand the paper back to the gnome.

He takes it and crumples up the paper in his hands, then tosses it into the fire. 'Now we release your wishes to the fire fairies, for they will transmute them into reality,' he says.

The gnome continues:

> *When we truly wish from our heart, there is much power. Now, see your wishes as if they are already granted. Feel it from the tip of your nose to your toes. Be receptive to any inspirations that come to you, and be prepared to put in the hard work, for this, my human friend, is a two-way street, and it is here that we will always meet.*

You nod to acknowledge his words of wisdom, and know that it is time to come back into the human world again. You get up and head towards the wooden door. You step over the threshold and find yourself back in the place where you started.

Ground yourself and write about your experiences in your fairy journal.

85

Cornish Knockers Meditation

ornish Knockers are a type of gnome found in mines in Cornwall. They are not as common today, as the mines are no longer in use. They get their name – Knockers – because they used to knock on the walls of the mines to warn the miners of any impending danger.

If you wish to connect with the Knockers, follow this simple meditation.

Close your eyes and visualize yourself standing at the entrance to a mine shaft. Ask for permission from the gnomes of the mines to enter. Wait a few moments and you will feel the answer.

A large, smiling gnome comes to greet you. He is holding a large, red hat, which he places upon your head. This is an extra layer of protection for you as you journey into the mine.

The gnome gestures to you to follow him down the stairs. There are lots of stairs, and you slowly start to walk down them, following the gnome, who is leading the way.

You count down with each step – 10, 9, 8, 7, 6, 5, 4, 3, 2, 1 – and find yourself at the bottom of the stairs. You feel safe, protected and loved, and know that the Knockers are protecting you and keeping you safe for the duration of this meditation.

You are greeted by a group of smiling gnomes. They are happy to welcome you to their domain.

There is a tiny golden cart, and you are invited to step inside and take a ride.

The cart takes you through the mine, where you see crystals and gold, glistening and shining. You have never seen a sight like this before. Riches as far as the eye can see.

The gnome says:

We can help you to attain riches within your human life – riches of the mind, body and soul, and if you are lucky, some material riches too.

The gnome then stops the golden cart and hands you a large, golden nugget, saying:

This is our gift for you, and is a sign we will always be true. Use this golden nugget to call upon us, day or night, and we will come to your aid if the need is sincere. Simply knock three times and we will hear.

Then, with a flash and a blink, they all disappear! You find yourself at the bottom of the stairs again, and you start to ascend – 1, 2, 3, 4, 5, 6, 7, 8, 9, 10. You are back at the top of the stairs once again!

You place the golden nugget into your pocket, and give thanks in your mind to the magical Cornish gnomes – the Knockers – knowing that you can call upon them again whenever you wish.

Remember to ground yourself to bring yourself back into your human reality.

86

Meet a Fairy Meditation

This is one of my 'go to' techniques to connect with fairies. It's super simple to follow and will open the door to fairy connections. Follow the steps in this magical meditation to meet a fairy.

Gather some fresh or dried flowers to represent nature and the realm of the fairies. Place them on your fairy altar (*see page 15*). Light a candle and burn some incense. You could also place some fairy or gnome figurines on your altar, if you have any.

Sit facing your altar. Close your eyes and imagine that you are walking along a garden path. You can smell the beautiful fragrance of the flowers and you can also see birds, butterflies and bumble bees flying around.

You notice a large oak tree at the end of the path, and you walk towards it and sit with your back against its trunk. You then say:

Fairies, fairies, come to me, as I sit beneath this tree. If it be your will, then please come and visit me. I ask this for the highest good of all beings, including myself.

Allow your mind to drift and be receptive to any signs of fairy activity. Let your imagination flow free. When fairies are near, they come with a different energy, which everyone experiences differently.

Remember that there are no rules by which fairies may present themselves to you. They may appear in disguise as small or large woodland creatures – for example, as birds, bees, butterflies or other insects. When a fairy comes near, you will instinctively know that the energy has changed. At this point, become receptive to any messages the fae may wish to impart.

Stay in this meditative space for as long as feels right – you'll instinctively know when it's time to open your eyes. Once you're ready, say thank you, then eat and drink something to help ground yourself.

Become a Fairy Ambassador

I was once invited to initiate a TV presenter into becoming a fairy ambassador live on television. The person took their role very seriously, actually, which was heartening – even though there were giggles galore! It was a touching and special moment.

To become a fairy ambassador, one needs to be mindful of how one treads upon the Earth. We must be aware of how we treat the planet; for example, by being aware of the household products we use, and swapping out products containing harmful chemicals for more natural, environmentally friendly ones.

We must also look at the things we personally consume when we eat or drink. Try to eat food that is organic, fresh and plant-based – and to drink pure mineral water, if possible. I know this is not realistic for everyone. Simply do your best in your particular circumstances.

For the initiation, you'll need a fairy wand (*see page 99*).

First, ground and protect yourself and use the 444 Breathing Technique (*see pages 9–13*).

Now for the fun part! Take your fairy wand and 'open' a fairy ring. To do this, simply draw an imaginary circle in the air with your wand. As you do this, visualize golden fairy dust and golden light coming from the tip of your wand. Draw the circle three times in a clockwise direction.

Then stand in the centre of the fairy ring, place your hand over your heart area, and say:

> *I declare that I will serve the fairies, in any way I can. By*
> *picking up litter, and by being mindful about how gently*
> *I tread upon the Earth. And I will do my best to spread*
> *love, light, joy and laughter, in every waking moment. This*
> *is my heartfelt pledge to the fairies. I will take my role as*
> *a fairy ambassador seriously and carry out this role to the*
> *best of my ability. I will have lots of fun doing it, too!*

Next, think about one practical thing you can do today to show your appreciation to the fae. Set your intention to do at least one such thing *every* day. Write about these in your fairy journal, along with anything else you recall about your experience.

Remember, we do not worship the fairies – we simply honour them for the work they selflessly do, as the guardians of nature.

88

Infinite Wishes Ritual

airies and wishes go hand-in-hand, making this the perfect ritual not only to manifest your wishes but also to connect with the fairies. Dandelions are known for their ability to produce infinite wishes from their magical seed heads (*see page 109*). Dandelions can be found in abundance in the wild, and provide food and nourishment for insects, animals and humans alike. Their delicate petals can be sprinkled on salads – in fact, the entire plant can be ingested in various ways.

Find a dandelion in seed. Ask for the plant's permission to pick the seed head, then carefully place it in a paper bag.

Take a special ceramic pot – you could either make this or buy it. Prepare some soil (ideally, organic soil with no pesticides)

and place it in the pot. Then place the pot on your fairy altar (*see page 15*), and light a white, unscented candle. Do this at the time of a full moon.

Take the seed head from the paper bag and hold it above the soil, saying:

> *Each seed here is a wish, yet to be fulfilled. From each wish springs forth another wish. With the blessings of the fairies of this land, I plant this wish, from my hand. Infinite wishes I nurture through seed, and water I shall, to fulfil the plant's need. With love and light, and all things bright, I care for this plant through my heart's delight. I plant this seed under the full moon's light.*

Then make a shallow hole in the soil, place the dandelion seed head inside the hole, and cover it with soil.

Tend the seeds daily, ensuring they are watered regularly, and place the pot outside when the weather is fine. Show love and kindness to the seeds as they germinate and grow into a dandelion plant. As the plant grows, you may wish to replant it outside. Ensure it gets adequate sunlight.

When the first flower blooms, ask for the plant's permission, then take some of its petals and sprinkle them on a salad. When the first seed heads form on the plant, place these in a magical jar. (This is a jar you have dedicated to your magical practices. Take any clean jar, and cleanse it by wafting burning sage over it as you state your intention that this jar will only be used for magical practices.)

Place the jar on your fairy altar (*see page 15*), where you keep sacred fairy things and wishes, for future use.

Say thank you to the spirit of the plant, and to the fairies for assisting you during this process.

89

Midsummer Night's Dream Spell

Many of us are familiar with William Shakespeare's *A Midsummer Night's Dream* – a play telling the tale of fairies playing games with humans on this most enchanted of nights! Midsummer's Eve is certainly a potent and magical time, during which fairies pierce the veil into our realm. This makes it the perfect time to connect with fairies.

This spell can be done indoors or outside. I always say that doing it outside is best. However, I know that this is not always possible, and doing it inside works equally well.

You'll need some fairy dust (biodegradable glitter), a white or light-coloured candle (ideally non-scented), a small jar or lantern if going outside and some rose essential oil and rose petals to represent midsummer.

The spell is to be performed any time between dusk and midnight on Midsummer's Eve.

Ground and protect yourself and use the 444 Breathing Technique (*see pages 9–13*).

If you are indoors, go to your fairy altar (*see page 15*). If you are outside, find a natural altar – perhaps next to a tree with a fairy door (*see page 79*), or somewhere else that calls to you.

Place a few drops of the rose essential oil in your palm and put a small dab onto your third eye area (between your eyebrows). Then pick up your candle and, using your index finger and thumb, rub the oil from the top to the bottom. As you do this, say:

> *I call upon Oberon and Titania, King and Queen of the fairies, to help me to love all that I see, and to accept with good grace what life gives to me. I call also on Puck, to bring me good luck and good fortune for ever more. I am knocking upon your fairy door.*

Next, light your candle, and say:

> *With this flame I ignite this spell, for the highest good of all, wishing everyone well.*

Then, sprinkle your fairy dust over the flame. Hear it crackle and pop as the energy rises. Take care when doing this and keep your face and eyes at a distance.

Next, take your rose petals, hold them up high and allow them to fall gently over your head, energizing you with their sweetly scented energy.

While you are doing all of this, hold the intention of inviting the King and Queen of the fairies to connect with you. Be mindful that Puck can and probably will play games, as he is prone to do!

90

Sense a Sylph Meditation

The fairies of the air are known as sylphs. They are in the breeze that blows through the trees, and in the gale that howls over the sea. They also dwell in the mind and imagination, and are the perfect allies to call upon for help in finding inspiration or reaching resolutions.

This meditation can be done indoors or outside. If you choose to do it indoors, open a window. Ideally, do it on a day or night when there is a slight to moderate breeze.

Prepare yourself using grounding and protection exercises and use the 444 Breathing Technique (*see pages 9–13*).

Get yourself into a comfortable position and close your eyes, then focus your attention on the breeze. Feel the beautiful sensation as it caresses your face and plays with your hair. Then say:

Fairies of the air, playing in the breeze. I wish upon the wind, come and go as you please. Blow peace and wisdom my way, dear fairies of the air. Trees swaying in the breeze, feel it in my heart, I care.

This simple, heartfelt request will attract the light and airy energy of the sylphs. Continue to meditate, while visualizing the sylphs flying around you, throwing clarity in the form of magical fairy dust. Allow your mind to flow as inspiration and imagination take over. Try not to judge what you feel or think, just allow it to simply 'be'.

Feel a sense of peace and calm wash over you. Send out gratitude from your heart into your environs. Do this by visualizing beautiful golden light emanating from your heart chakra, radiating out as far as you can imagine.

When you feel ready, open your eyes and ground yourself by eating a piece of bread, some fruit or a biscuit. Even connecting briefly with the fairies of the air can make you feel a little light-headed, so taking extra care to ground yourself is essential.

Cottingley Fairy Experiment

f you love fairies, then chances are you'll have heard of the Cottingley Fairies. This is the case of two young cousins, Frances Griffiths and Elsie Wright, who supposedly 'fooled' writer Sir Arthur Conan Doyle – and the rest of the world – with their photographs of cut-out fairies more than a hundred years ago.

I was fortunate to interview Christine Lynch, the daughter of Frances Griffiths, for *FAE* magazine. She told me that her mother had said that all of the photographs were fake, except for the fifth one, which she insisted was real.

The story inspired me so much that I encouraged readers of *FAE* magazine to create their own Cottingley-inspired photographs, and I dedicated an extra-special edition to this magical story.

So, why not try your own Cottingley-inspired fairy experiment? Take some paints, pencils or crayons and draw some fairies. They do not have to be perfect – just allow your imagination to flow freely. Think about the Cottingley cut-out fairies, which fooled even Sir Arthur Conan Doyle all those years ago.

Draw a few fairies, then carefully cut them out. Find some lollipop sticks and tape them to the backs of the fairy art. Then go outside and place the fairies in the grass, or somewhere in nature. At the bottom of the garden would be ideal for this.

Then grab your camera and take some photographs. If you have a friend you can do this with, even better. But if not, it's just as much fun as a solo experiment.

As you place the fairies and take the photos, posing for them yourself if you wish, say:

> *Cottingley fairies, forever held in time, I call to your fairy spirits, so sweet and divine. Enchant these photos with your bright shining light, I call to your fairy spirits, this is your invite. Always for the highest good of all, and harming none, always for the highest good, now let us have some fun!*

As you create your scene, imagine being one of the Cottingley children, playing make-believe, then finding out it was real!

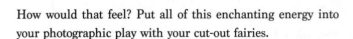

How would that feel? Put all of this enchanting energy into your photographic play with your cut-out fairies.

When you have finished, print out the photos if you can, and place them, along with your cut-out fairies, on your fairy altar (*see page 15*). The local fairies will be curious about them for sure!

©BH Hawkins

92

Fairy Fragrance

This is an interesting one. My first experience of fairy fragrance occurred while I was in some local woodland, preparing to do one of my regular fairy oracle readings. I was deep in the woods, when suddenly I smelt toffee apples! The smell was so sweet and uplifting. I knew it was a fairy fragrance as there was no one else around, and it was such a distinctive and unusual smell to experience in that setting. It took me back to my childhood, when I first encountered fairies.

I had heard of the spirits of relatives coming through with a fragrance, often in the form of a perfume. But I did not learn until later that this phenomenon is known as clairalience – the ability to perceive spirits, and fairies, through your sense of smell.

When I got home later that day, I tuned in to the fairies during a meditation, and asked them what the smell was.

They instantly replied, 'It's a personalized calling card for you. It's another way you can tell we are near.'

It was such a beautiful encounter, unlike any I'd had before. So, I thought it would be fun to include it in this book.

Ideally, you will need to be outside for this, although, as I sit here writing these words indoors, I can smell a waft of toffee apples! I assume this is the fairies' way of saying that you can be indoors too!

It's important NOT to burn incense or scented candles, for the obvious reason that it could interfere with the spirit-smells from the fairies. Ideally, have the window open, if you are inside, to air the room.

Prepare yourself using grounding and protection exercises, then use the 444 Breathing Technique (*see pages 9–13*).

When you are ready to begin, say the following:

> *The sweetest of smells, is the most magical of calling*
> *cards. Enliven my senses and share your enchanting*
> *scent with me. Show me you are here, show me you*
> *are near, with your beautiful fairy fragrance.*

The thing with this exercise is that you cannot force it – you will either smell something or you won't. It will be very apparent if you do. If nothing happens the first time, simply try again, ideally leaving a week or so between attempts.

If you *do* experience a fragrance, it will probably rekindle a memory, so make a note of this in your fairy journal. Or, if you're not sure whether you smelled anything, make a note of that, too.

93

Telepathic Talking

eveloping telepathic awareness is a powerful way to connect and communicate with fairies. Fairies often communicate telepathically with words, thoughts, feelings and colours. Fairies have been communicating with me in this way for many years. I simply hear them in my mind. I know this isn't my own internal voice, because it has a very different 'sound' and a different feeling about it.

Back in 2006, I was guided telepathically by the fairies to start my 3 Wishes Fairy Festival. The communication came across very boldly, with a bit of a bossy tone! 'You must organize a festival,' it said! Well, that certainly caught my attention as I would never speak to myself in that manner! It continued, 'It must be in Cornwall at the time of Midsummer, and you must announce it now!'

Wow! As you can imagine, this felt like a direct and powerful instruction. Remember that we all have the power to say no to any external instructions, no matter what dimension they are from. I sat and thought about this instruction for a short time, tuned into my gut, and decided it sounded like a fun thing to do. So, I replied, 'Yes!' It really felt like the right thing to do, and in retrospect, I'm so glad I agreed to it.

Telepathic guidance can often lead to beautiful manifestations. However, there must also be a proviso here, as fairies can sometimes lead us down what I like to call the pixie-path! In both scenarios, there are lessons to be learned, and trusting your own instincts is paramount.

Here is a fun exercise to try if you would like to attempt telepathic communication with the fairies.

First, get into a comfortable position. Use your grounding and protection techniques and use the 444 Breathing Technique (see *pages 9–13*). If you are able to do this exercise somewhere outside in nature, all the better, but it can be done anywhere. If you are indoors, then being next to a plant will enhance the fairy connection.

In your mind, send out an easy-to-answer question to the fairies. You can do this by silently saying words in your mind, or if you are more of a visual person, then create images using your imagination while focusing on the fairies. It could start something like this:

Fairies, if you can hear me, please answer telepathically. My question is simple, so answer me do, and I will reply telepathically to you!

Await a reply, trying not to form an answer inside your mind. A response from the fairies will rarely come in the way that you expect it to – always expect the unexpected! Be open to the many and varied ways a response can arise. It could be a voice (other than your own). It will be obvious to you if this does happen, as you know what your own internal dialogue sounds like and will be able to recognise it. A fairy reply can also come as a sound, a vision, a fragrance or as colours. Be aware that fairy time is not the same as our sense of time, so the response may come right away or hours, days or even weeks down the line!

I would suggest trying this exercise for seven days in a row to see what, if anything, happens.

Remember to document your experiences in your fairy journal as this will be helpful later as you deepen and explore your connection with the fairies. Over time, you will start to see patterns in the things that work best for you.

94

Magical Mushrooms Meditation

We often see magical mushrooms and toadstools depicted in fairy art, as they are synonymous with the fairy realm. Fungi have an otherworldly and mystical appeal. Have you ever watched nature documentaries, in which mushrooms and toadstools are shown growing and spreading their spores? It really is quite incredible and very magical to watch. So, I thought it would be fun to include a magical mushroom meditation.

First, find an image of mushrooms in a fairy ring, and we shall meditate on this. The meditation can be done indoors or outside. If outside, then during autumn would be wonderful, as you're likely to see many varieties of fungi growing on tree stumps in the woods or in fairy rings.

To prepare, find a safe and quiet space where you can sit down comfortably and use the 444 Breathing Technique (*see page 9*). Look at the image of the fairy ring, so this imagery will be fresh in your mind, then close your eyes.

Visualize the mycelium (fungi roots) growing deep down into the earth. This will help you to ground and to connect with the energy of the fungi, and their fairy guardians.

Visualize a fairy ring consisting of several mushrooms. Notice the shapes and colours and any smells associated with them. Just 'be' with this energy for a few moments.

After a while, you notice the tiniest movements, and you see that the mushrooms' umbrella-like caps start tilting backwards to reveal adorable fairy faces. Each face is different, and they're all smiling.

One of the magical mushrooms gestures for you to come closer. Know that you are always safe, protected and loved as you make your way towards the mushroom-being. 'I have a magical message for you,' says the smiling fungus! Be conscious of any message, word or image that floats into your mind. It might not make sense, but remember that fairies and their mushroom allies speak in their own language.

You say thank you, and slowly move back to your starting position, feeling your body against the grass, ground, floor or chair where you're sitting. Wriggle your toes and fingers, roll your shoulders, and when you feel ready, open your eyes.

Take a few moments, then grab your fairy journal and write down any experiences or magical messages you may have received. If you can't recall anything, that's totally fine – you can always do this meditation again, as you'll be more familiar with the process and more receptive to any messages and signs.

95

Away with the Fairies Meditation

ver since I was a young child, I've been told that I am 'away with the fairies'! I have always taken this as a compliment, although I realize that it is probably not always meant to be! The saying usually refers to someone who is not fully present, here in this reality. Well, I admit that this has always been true for me. I have always stood with one foot in the earthly realm and the other in Fairyland. So, it felt right for me to share this 'Away with the Fairies' meditation.

Get yourself comfortable in a place where you will not be disturbed. You can play soft music, light a candle and burn incense, if you wish. Then ground and protect yourself and use the 444 Breathing Technique (*see pages 9–13*).

When you feel fully relaxed, close your eyes and visualize yourself in a beautiful garden.

There are vibrant fairy lights darting around, as if they are excited to see you. The fairy lights start to fly around your head and you can hear giggling.

You begin to smile and giggle, too. There is much excitement on both sides for the journey that is about to come.

The fairy lights fly faster and faster around you, until they start to take the form of fairies, wearing iridescent, gossamer gowns, with wings like insects'. It's a magical scene to behold.

The fairies move in closer and reach out their hands to you. You reach out and accept them. Before you know it, you are floating upwards, higher and higher, to the sound of the giggling fairies, who say:

> *We are the fairies who have come to take you away! Not for an hour, not for a day, just for a short time, so we can show you our land, so hold on tightly, dear human, for this is our land.*

How could you refuse such a magical invitation? Surrendering to the fairies, you allow them to fly you over their realm, pointing out the different trees, plants, shrubs and flowers. You are experiencing a fairy's-eye view, and it is beautiful.

You can feel your giggling fairy guides' passion and love for the land as you fly high above it with them.

Slowly and gently, the fairies start to descend back to the Earth, and before you know it, you are back in the place where you first started! The fairies say:

> *We will see you again soon, human friend.*
> *Until that time, our love we do send.*

And with that, you become aware of your body again. When you feel ready, open your eyes and make sure you ground yourself by having a little nibble of food.

96

Water Fairies Meditation

Have you ever noticed a magical energy when you are close to a river, stream, lake or waterfall? This is very common in places where there is flowing fresh water. The fairies of the water have a different and very magical quality and it is truly tangible in these places.

Go outside to a place where there is a stream, waterfall or other source of flowing fresh water. Taking care, get yourself close enough to the water to feel the 'chi' – the life-force energy of the water. If you can get close enough to feel the water droplets or water spray on your skin, even better. You could also do this inside your home, simply by sitting next to a running cold-water tap.

Do your grounding and protection exercises and use the 444 Breathing Technique *(see pages 9–13)*. You'll probably find that relaxation comes more swiftly when you are next to flowing fresh water.

Say:

> *Fairies of the water, I feel you are near, as the mist caresses my*
> *skin and the water vapour permeates the air. I come as a child,*
> *open-hearted and without care. Your cleansing, watery energy*
> *pours over me now. I see you out of the corner of my eye, swinging*
> *from the bough. I hear a distant giggle, or was it the water's rush?*
> *I see you in my mind's eye, saying 'gently, human, hush…'.*

Sit in silent meditation for as long as feels right, paying attention to your environment and noticing anything out of the ordinary. After the exercise, make a note of anything you experienced in your fairy journal.

97

Mermaid and
Mer-Fairy Ritual

f you follow me on social media, then you'll know that I connect with all elementals, including the mermaids and mer-fairies. So, I just had to share this enchanting oceanic ritual with you.

If you're able to visit a beach for this ritual, that would be perfect. However, I realize this won't be possible for everyone, and I have devised this ritual so that anyone can connect with the mer-beings, whether they are inland or close to the sea.

Get some pure water – ideally from a natural spring, or mineral or filtered water. Next, get some salt – ideally natural salt with no additives, as many salt products have anti-caking agent in them.

Find a lovely container – perhaps a ceramic or glass bowl. If you have an aquamarine container that reminds you of the ocean, that would be ideal, but it isn't essential.

Do your grounding and protection exercises and use the 444 Breathing Technique (*see pages 9–13*).

Put a few pinches of the salt into the container. Then put your clean fingers into the water and let the drips fall onto the salt. Stir the salt and water together, while saying the following:

> *With water and salt, to symbolize 'sea', may mer-fairy*
> *wisdom reside within me. So it is, and so 'shell' it be.*

Close your eyes and place your finger onto your third eye area (between your eyebrows). Feel the energy of the salt water cleansing your third eye, and energetically connecting you to the mer-beings. Sit for a while and absorb this beautiful energy. Allow your mind to drift and see what floats into it.

When you feel ready, open your eyes and ground yourself. Drink some water (not the salt water!), then put the water in your container outside, or place it on your fairy altar (*see page 15*) and let it evaporate.

After this exercise, ensure you drink water regularly. Drinking water will keep you connected to this energy, and it's good for your physical body, too.

98

Connecting with Fairies of Ancient Stones

he fairies of ancient stones can be fiercely protective. This makes total sense – after all, the stones are their home. In much the same way as we humans gravitate towards these ancient places, so too do the fairies. There is a sense of sacredness and deep peace to be found there.

I recall a time when I was visiting a place called Dolmen de la Grotte aux Fées in France. It is a megalithic monument made of large, stone slabs which – legend has it – were placed there by fairies (*fées* means fairies in French). I discovered this place through a book titled *The Sun and the Serpent*, by Paul Broadhurst and Hamish Millar. In this book, the pair dowsed ley lines in the UK and Europe and discovered that there is a ley line going through the Dolmen de la Grotte aux Fées. So, naturally, I had to visit!

I thought the French fairies would be happy to welcome a fairy ambassador from the UK, so I went merrily on my way, in a van with a friend.

I presumed that because I had come all the way from England, I would receive a warm fairy welcome. Alas, that was not the case! It was nighttime when we arrived, and there was an eerie feeling in the area. It did not feel welcoming at all. In fact, it felt quite the opposite.

Still, I bravely approached the Dolmen stones, and from a distance, I could see lots of shining, luminous green eyes peeking out from them. Then, telepathically, I heard a very loud and clear 'NO!' It literally stopped me in my tracks!

I was very surprised to be told no – especially as I had travelled all the way from the UK, and I love and work with fairies all the time. It just didn't feel right. However, if the fairies say 'no' in such a bold and commanding manner, it is wise to heed their advice. So we headed back to the van and decided to find somewhere else to park up for the night, while we contemplated our next move.

We were driving for ages, but the roads and scenery started to look familiar. If I'm totally honest, it felt a bit spooky! We continued driving, only to find that we were going round in circles, and every road we took led us back to the same place.

We were still in the aura of Dolmen de la Grotte aux Fées, and we were getting nowhere fast! Eventually, we decided to stop and park up for the evening.

The next morning, around dawn, I was awoken by a voice saying, 'You can come now!'

I was feeling tired, and thought about going back to sleep, but I knew this was one invitation I had to accept right away. I woke my friend, told him about the mystical message I'd just received and said that we needed to head to the stones right away. Interestingly, as we approached them in the dawn light, the area felt a lot friendlier, and we both felt welcomed. We ended up spending the entire day there.

I was confused by my initial experience at the stones, so I meditated and asked the fairies why they had refused us entry at nighttime. This was their reply:

> *You approached our sacred home in the nighttime hours.*
> *We did not know what your intention was, so we needed*
> *to scan your energy first. Many people come here and do*
> *not respect it, so we are very protective of this space.*

Now I understood, and this is why I am sharing this story with you. We must always respect not only ancient stones, but all sacred and ancient places where fairies are known to dwell. Only attempt to connect with fairies of these places if you have the wisdom to listen to them, and never assume you are welcome.

If you still wish to connect with the fairies of ancient stones, go in the daytime initially, and walk around the monument three times in a clockwise direction. Announce your arrival, perhaps by saying your name out loud and giving your reason or intention for visiting the place. The fairies will then 'scan' your energy. Then wait – wait for a clear yes or no, and do not take it too personally (like I did!) if their first answer is no.

Imagine if someone knocked on your door in the middle of the night. If you did not know them, would you welcome them in with open arms? No! You would want to know who they were and why they were knocking on your door!

If the fairies' answer is yes, then proceed with reverence and be receptive to any signs or messages you receive while you are there. When you depart, leave a gift to thank the fairies – something biodegradable, such as a flower, fresh fruit or a strand of hair.

99

The Fairy King of Glastonbury Tor Meditation

This meditation is special to me because I host many of my fairy events in Glastonbury. I have forged my own connection with the King of the Fairies, and ask for his blessings when I bring fairy celebrations to the town.

There are several differing stories about the Fairy King, or Gwynn ap Nudd (pronounced *Gwynn ap Nuth*). According to folklore, the Fairy King is said to reside in a glass castle inside Glastonbury Tor. Glastonbury (derived from *Glass-town-borough*) was once an island surrounded by water, known as the Isle of Glass. My own theory is that the symbolic glass castle inside the Tor stems from the mythical Arthurian island of Avalon, which has often been identified as the former island of Glastonbury Tor. Whatever the truth about this is, my intuition feels the Fairy King in this enchanted space. The energy at the top of the Tor is tangible and powerful. It feels like a very magical place, and many spiritual seekers are drawn there.

I have devised this simple meditation to meet with the King inside the Tor. The meditation can be done on the Tor itself, or from your home – if you're at home, all you'll need is an image of Glastonbury Tor as a focus for your meditation.

Find a comfortable and quiet place for the meditation. Have the image of Glastonbury Tor in front of you – either on your fairy altar (*see page 15*) or resting on the floor or on a table. Or, if you are familiar with Glastonbury Tor, you can simply hold the vision of it inside your mind.

Prepare yourself using grounding and protection techniques and use the 444 Breathing Technique (*see pages 9–13*).

Close your eyes. Visualize yourself sitting at the top of the Tor. Feel the powerful hill beneath you, and feel the energy pulsing through it, rising up from below. Visualize this energy as golden light, entering your body and forming a protective shield.

A ladder appears before you. It reaches down into the Tor through a glass door. You climb onto the ladder and start climbing downwards, counting backwards with each rung, from 10 to one.

As you reach one, you find yourself standing in front of a large glass door. You say:

> *I have travelled to meet with the Fairy King, may I*
> *enter and be with him? I come in peace and love.*

A fairy guide opens the door and asks you, 'Why have you come to this place? What is your purpose?'

Reply instinctively, from your heart. If you are lost for words, you could say something like:

> *I wish to meet with the Fairy King, for the highest good of all, that*
> *he may share with me that which I need to know. I am the eternal*
> *student, forever in the eternal flow. I come in peace and love.*

The guide steps to one side and gestures for you to enter through the glass door into the castle where the Fairy King resides.

You walk along a long, glass-floored corridor until you reach the throne room. Upon the throne sits the Fairy King. He stares at you with icy eyes, then suddenly starts to laugh! You're not sure what to do, until he invites you to sit before him.

You both sit in silence for a while, then he says:

Brave is the one who seeks me out. You have faced your fear to be here, and for that I applaud you. For you know not what to expect. You have trusted your heart, and therefore, an audience is hereby granted. Ask me what you wish, and reply I may.

Allow your question to flow from your heart, not your mind, and speak with love.

Take a few moments to allow a conversation between yourself and the Fairy King. He may not answer in words – he may answer with a feeling, a thought may pop into your mind or you may hear him telepathically. You may also see a symbol. Receive any communication with gratitude and love.

You bow your head to the Fairy King and slowly walk backwards, facing the King at all times. The guide then gently taps you on the shoulder and leads you back to the glass door and the ladder, where you start to climb back up to the top of the Tor. Count from one to 10 until you are safely back at the top again.

When you feel ready, open your eyes and write in your fairy journal straight away, including everything you have just experienced.

Ground yourself again, have a bite to eat and drink some water. If you are in Glastonbury, you could drink water from the White Spring that flows from inside the Tor. This will strengthen your connection to the Fairy King and with the Tor.

100

Look in the Leaves

airies often shapeshift, and one of their favourite ways to do this is to disguise themselves in the leaves. This fun magical practice is best done during the autumn months, when the leaves are falling from the trees.

Go outside to a wooded area or a place with several leafy trees. Simply walk amongst the trees, looking down at the fallen leaves, and notice any fairy-like features or faces. I find this works best if you allow your eyes to go into fairy-focus, and by this I mean to go into a soft gaze. Allow your intuition to guide you in where to look.

It might take some time, or a few walks, before you start seeing fairy faces in the leaves. Once you do see one, you'll know it – they'll start popping up everywhere like mushrooms! This is a form of fairy sight (*see page 269*).

Acknowledge the fairy faces when you see them by saying a simple hello, or smiling. Show the fairies that you are a friend and not a foe.

You may wish to take a photo of the faces on your phone, but do not use a flash, as this will disturb the fairies' energy. Ideally, keep the memory in your heart. If you do wish to take photographs, it may be useful to read the entry about photographing fairies first (*see page 71*).

Do not disturb the leaves, especially when you do see fairy faces in them. Moving the leafy formations can disturb the fairies' energy.

101

Find Fairy Faces
in the Trees

f you enjoyed the Look in the Leaves exercise in the previous entry, then you'll love this. I find that spotting fairy faces in the trees is much easier than spotting them amongst fallen leaves.

The fairies of the trees may also be called tree dryads, or devas. Their faces are often gnarly and characterful.

As you did for the Look in the Leaves exercise, go outside to a wooded area or a place with several trees – except this time, you can go at any time of year, not just in the autumn.

Wander around the wooded area, looking at the trees but trying not to look *too* hard, if that makes sense. Allow your eyes to go into fairy-focus (go into a soft gaze). Then simply allow your gaze to flow where it will.

At some point, your gaze will be drawn to what appears to be a fairy face.

When this happens, simply say hello or smile to acknowledge the tree-being. If it feels especially friendly, you may even wish to hug the tree. Always ask the tree's permission before doing this, though. Do this by asking telepathically, or out loud if it feels appropriate, 'Tree, may I connect with you?' Then wait for a feeling – perhaps the fairy fizzes (*see page 121*), or just an inner-knowing – to give you your answer.

Once you see one fairy face in a tree, you'll probably start seeing them everywhere you look.

You may wish to take some photographs of the faces you see in the trees, but do not use a flash, as this will disturb their energy. You could include any photographs – or perhaps sketches of your findings – in your fairy journal.

Fairy Sight

omeone who has the gift of fairy sight – also known as a fairy-seer – is a person who is *au fait* (excuse the pun!) with the fairy realm and who can see and communicate with fairies easily. This ability can develop naturally, although it usually takes many months or even years of practice.

This ability is not dissimilar to that of clairvoyance or mediumship, except that the person is developing the ability to connect with the fairy realm, rather than with departed spirits. There are a few respected teachers in this field who will impart their knowledge – usually for an energy exchange, a donation or a fee (interesting, as the French word for fairy is *fée*!).

If you are interested in receiving such teaching, simply put forth your request to the fairies, asking for the perfect teacher to manifest so that you can deepen your connection with the fairies. It is said that when the student is ready, the teacher will appear. Sometimes, the teacher will find you and sometimes you will find the teacher. There is no right or wrong way for this to happen.

You could say something like this:

> *Fairies, please place a fairy-seer upon my path, so that I may see*
> *you as clearly as they. I ask from my heart and for the highest*
> *good of all beings. I trust that this guide will appear in the perfect*
> *place and at the perfect time. So it is and so shall it be.*

Then simply be receptive and open to any 'chance' meetings you may have. After all, it's not every day you'll come across a true fairy-seer.

103

Find a Fairy House

Back in 2019, I found the sweetest fairy house in a tree trunk – complete with a door and window. I was so enchanted that I asked my friend to film me showing it and talking about it. I uploaded the video to my YouTube channel and it went viral! This tells me that people are genuinely captivated by fairy houses. There is something extra magical about them.

So, how do you go about finding a fairy house? Well, you use your imagination and all of your eyes – including your third eye! Knowing where to find a fairy house comes down to a feeling, and an intuitive hunch.

I suggest walking in a wooded area, and noticing the trees. See where you are drawn.

If you have a dog, perhaps take it with you, as animals have a sixth sense for fairies and fairy houses. You could literally take your dog's lead (excuse the pun!).

You could also use your sixth sense and divine a fairy house. Use your whole body and all of your senses like a fairy dowsing branch (*see page 275*) to lead you to a fairy house. Alternatively, you could bring your own dowsing branch or find one on the woodland floor.

Things to look out for:

* gnarly trees, which look as though they have windows and doors

* signs of fairy homes in the undergrowth – perhaps a twig sticking up that looks like a miniature chimney pot

* toadstools and mushrooms, as these often grow near fairy abodes

Remember that fairy dwellings do not always look like conventional human homes, though they often do. As I frequently say in this book, expect the unexpected, for in the fairy realm everything is inside out, upside down and betwixt and between!

Never touch or disturb a fairy house, as this will disturb and upset the fairies, and also the insects and wild animals that fairies sometimes share their homes with.

104

Make a
Fairy Dwelling

reating your own fairy house is a wonderful way to connect with the fairies. Plus, you can place it in your fairy garden, if you have one (*see page 95*). You'll probably discover signs of magical new residents pretty much immediately.

You do not need to be a master sculptor or professional craftsperson to make a fairy house. You can create one from pretty much anything! Just be sure that the house is made from natural materials with no harsh chemicals.

The beauty of creating with and for the fairies is that you can allow your creative side to lead the way. And if you feel stuck, you can simply ask the fairies for guidance and inspiration, saying:

*I am building you a fairy house, where you can live, work
and play. This home is built from love and light, joy and
laughter, and all things right. I trust in your new home, you
will delight. I am open to guidance, so feel free to inspire.
My heart and mind are open, for your wish is my desire!*

Gather natural materials, such as pebbles, pieces of wood,
crystals, stones, straw, twigs and so on. Do not cut any living
plant or tree to create the house: use only things that have
fallen naturally. You could perhaps use soil, straw and water
as mud 'cement': the same materials that 'cob' houses are
created from.

You could make tiny curtains and other accessories for your
fairy house, too. There is no end to the creative fun that may
be had when making a dwelling for the fairies.

105

Dowsing for Fairies

ave you heard of water divining, where a person can locate water by walking over an area with a Y-shaped branch or set of dowsing rods until the branch or set of rods twitches? Well, dowsing for fairies is similar. And some people can simply use their bodies to dowse for fairies!

Find a small, Y-shaped branch that has fallen naturally from a tree. This is your fairy dowsing branch. You could use dowsing rods, if you prefer. However, it's best not to use metal rods for finding fairies, as it is said that some (but not all) fairies dislike metal.

Before you start, do your grounding and protection exercises and use the 444 Breathing Technique (*see pages 9-13*).

Then go outside with your chosen divining tool. If you are using a Y-shaped branch, hold the top parts of the 'Y' in both hands with the long part pointing downwards as your guide.

Just walk intuitively. Let your heart and soul lead the way. Set your intention to find the fae, saying:

> *I seek you, fairies of this land, with this dowsing branch in my hand. May it lead me to where you dwell, if you wish me to find you, then my dowsing branch tell! For I will follow wherever it leads, and should I discover you, tell me your needs.*

Simply walk along, allowing yourself to be guided. You may 'divine' other things, such as water. Remember, though, that there are fairies who dwell by streams. Be open to all possibilities and enjoy the experience.

Fire Fairies Meditation

Fire elementals include fire fairies, salamanders and other fiery beings. Connecting with them can happen in a few different ways.

Flame divination is one way – and probably one of the safest ways. As with other forms of divination, it's a spiritual tool that may be helpful for seeing the flow of energy in your life. You simply gaze at the flames of a fire or a candle flame and notice any shapes that appear, along with any insights, thoughts and feelings that may arise.

You could also meet the fire elementals by walking on fire! Yes, you read that right! Firewalking is not for everyone, and must only be attempted under the very strict supervision of a qualified firewalking practitioner.

I walked on fire and it was an empowering experience for me. It made me feel that if I can walk on fire, I can do anything! It was amazing to see how my body instinctively knew how to protect itself.

If you do decide to try firewalking, then I stress again that it must always, always, always be done with professional guidance. It is also essential that you have the correct equipment, including a hose to wash down your feet with cold water after the walk, to ensure there are no embers present.

The following firewalking meditation can be done without the need for any real fire, which is far safer for you!

Ground and protect yourself and use the 444 Breathing Technique (*see pages 9–13*).

Visualize yourself standing on the threshold of a path of burning embers. There is smoke rising and you can feel the heat against your face and body. Say to yourself, 'I am safe, protected and loved at all times.' As you prepare to do the fire walk, hold the thought, or say out loud:

> *Fire fairies, I wish to connect with you, for the highest good of all. In safety I walk upon the flame, feeling safe and protected in this fiery domain.*

Then proceed to walk at a comfortable pace. Imagine feeling the heat of the hot embers. It does not hurt – it actually feels nice, and you feel empowered. When you have finished walking across the hot coals, allow yourself to celebrate this amazing achievement, then continue your meditation by sitting silently and saying:

I have walked upon the fire, to meet you in your domain. I have walked upon the fire, and felt the heat from the naked flame. It's an honour to meet you, fire fairies, and I hope you feel the same.

When you feel ready, you'll probably need to rest, as it can take a lot of energy to do this exercise. Write about your experience in your fairy journal, as it is likely to be a powerful one.

Create a Map
of Fairyland

reating your own map of Fairyland ties in naturally with dowsing and carrying out a fairy census (*see pages 275 and 282*). Tapping into your own creativity for this fun and magical project will undoubtedly delight the fairies.

There is a beautiful map of Fairyland called 'An Ancient Mappe of Fairyland', drawn by English artist Bernard Sleigh in 1917. It was on display at the British Library's Fantasy: Realms of the Imagination exhibition (2023/24), although, as you and I know, fairies are not fantasy – they are as real as real can be! You can view this breathtaking map online.

You can create your own map of the Fairyland terrain. Start by mapping out your local area, then expand upon it as you feel more confident. Mark points of interest, where there have been documented fairy sightings, or where you have personally experienced fairies. You could use your fairy dowsing branch in this exercise.

You might find that fairy activity tends to occur close to, or on, ley lines – usually straight energetic lines between significant historic structures, sites and landmarks. Mapping sites of fairy activity will certainly help to reveal any patterns, so will help you to predict where fairies may appear in the future.

You could also ask the fairies to tell you where you can see them next. You could say:

> *Fairies, as I map this land, show me where you'll be next. Let me know from you first-hand, so it's written in this text.*

108

Carry Out a Fairy Census

arrying out your own fairy census is a fun thing to do and links nicely with the Map of Fairyland exercise from the previous entry. When people tell you about their fairy experiences for your census, you could add reference points correlating with the fairy sightings on your map.

Once you start talking to people about your own fairy experiences, you'll find that many people have their own tales to tell. People can be shy about coming forward with their fairy stories for fear of being ridiculed or laughed at. It is worth reassuring them that you believe them, so they know they are safe to share their experiences with you.

You could make a confidential document, containing first names only, so that contributors cannot be identified, and keep it for personal use only. You'll probably find that your friends and family members have all experienced some form of fairy sighting. Treat finding out about these sightings as a fun experiment. You'll be like a private fairy investigator (PFI)!

Some of the details you may wish to include in your fairy census are:

* the date and time of day

* the age and gender of the person

* any significant astrological events; for example, a solar eclipse, a full moon or a comet sighting

* a description of the experience, sharing as much detail as possible

You could get your census printed up into a mini booklet by your local printers, or print a copy yourself.

So what does this have to do with connecting with fairies? Well, it will begin to give you a fairy-flavour of what people in your area are experiencing, and as you record these, you'll see patterns start to form. Perhaps sightings tend to happen at a full moon in woodland, for example.

109

Hawthorn Tree
Fairy Portals

The hawthorn has long been identified as a fairy tree. In Celtic lands, it is still remarked that lone hawthorns conceal doorways to the fairy realm, and are home to the 'good folk'. The hawthorn is a portal to Fairyland – its leaves, flowers and berries are all gateways to the fairy realm.

Thomas the Rhymer, the ephemeral mystic and poet, is said to have met the Queen of Elfland beneath the boughs of a hawthorn tree (known as the Eildon Tree) in the Scottish Borders. Thomas was enchanted by the Queen, and followed her under the tree and deep within the hill to Fairyland.

Always approach hawthorn trees, and indeed other sacred trees, with reverence and respect. Ask for nothing, except perhaps, in this instance, a glimpse of these magical fairy beings. Always take a gift as a token of your appreciation, to leave at the base of the tree trunk. Something organic, sweet and biodegradable makes the perfect offering.

This magical practice ideally needs to be done outside in nature. In theory, you could do it inside your home, but it is not likely to be as potent – unless you are well-versed in astral travel, but that's a whole other practice (*see page 146*)!

Locate a hawthorn tree, choosing when to do this according to the moon phase and season. During a full moon, with its strong moonlight, will be best and also most practical, as it will help you see where you are walking. You could choose to do it when the tree is in blossom or in berry. Trust your instinct as to the best time to go.

Ground and protect yourself and use the 444 Breathing Technique (*see pages 9–13*). Ask the tree for its permission to approach – do this by asking out loud or telepathically in your mind. Then wait for a response. This may be felt as an instant gut feeling of 'yes' or 'no', or you may even hear the answer in your mind. Sit as close to the tree as possible. It's best to keep your eyes open for the duration of this exercise, so you can observe any happenings.

Say out loud:

> *Fairies of this hawthorn tree, show me what you wish me to see. With an open heart and an open mind, I come in love, from humankind. My wish is to connect with you, tell me what I need to do.*

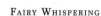
Now sit and practise your pixie-patience! Keep your eyes open and observe your surroundings. Notice any subtle or not-so-subtle movements. *If* the fairies wish to present themselves, they will, so the (fairy) ball really is in their court!

If you see a berry or a piece of blossom on the ground, ask for permission to take it home for your fairy altar (*see page 15*), as this will strengthen your connection with the hawthorn tree, and with the fairies who reside within it or close by.

Leave your gift, then make your way home. Write about anything you observed in your fairy journal, as this will be a lasting reminder of your experience with the hawthorn tree.

Connect with Fairies for Healing

I t is possible to connect with the fairies of love and light for the purpose of healing, and for improving your wellbeing. What follows is a simple fairy healing meditation.

Find a comfortable place where you will not be disturbed. You could either sit or lie down. You may wish to light a candle and burn some incense or sage.

Next, do your grounding and protection exercises, followed by the 444 Breathing Technique (*see pages 9–13*). With each inhale, breathe in love, light and healing energy; with each exhale, release any cares and concerns. Repeat this four times.

Close your eyes. Visualize yourself in a peaceful landscape, next to a small waterfall. A flutter of fairies, all dressed in iridescent white robes, slowly form a circle around you. This is your fairy protection ring. It will keep you safe, protected and loved for the duration of the healing meditation.

A few of the fairies fly over to the waterfall and cup their hands to catch some of the freshly flowing water. They fly back to the circle and hover above you, allowing the water to flow through their fairy fingers and gently onto the crown of your head.

You can feel the healing water slowly trickling down your head and over your body. Everywhere it touches feels renewed and energized.

You say to the fairies:

> *I receive this healing energy with grace and love, I accept the path of healing as it pours from above. Bless me with your presence, bless me with your light, bless me with your magic, as I sleep through the night.*

As you say this, the fairies move closer and golden fairy dust emanates from the palms of their hands, and towards your heart area. As the fairy dust touches you, you can feel the fairy fizzes all over your body (*see page 121*). You feel re-energized and renewed.

The fairies then say:

> *Our healing work is done here, it's time for us to disappear. We shall return another day, but for now, we must fly away.*

They smile and turn to wave. Then you watch them fly high up into the sky.

Spend a few moments enjoying this energy. Then start to wriggle your fingers and toes, roll your shoulders and sit in an upright position. When you feel ready, open your eyes. Do not get up too quickly as you may feel a little light-headed after this healing fairy experience.

Ensure that you are grounded and have a bite to eat. Take some time to rest, if you are able to. Otherwise, take things super slowly as your mind and body acclimatize to the healing energy you have just received. Try not to do anything too strenuous after this healing experience.

Connect with Fairies
for Manifesting

onnecting with fairies for the purpose of manifesting is something that is close to my heart. When we form a friendship with the fairies, they can – if they wish – help us to manifest inner and outer states of being, feelings and material things.

What follows is a meditation for manifesting.

Find a comfortable position, either in your home or outside in nature. Do your grounding and protection exercises, then close your eyes and breathe deeply, using the 444 Breathing Technique (*see pages 9–13*).

Visualize a magical garden, with lush green grass. Fragrance fills the air and the sun is shining. You feel a deep sense of peace as you relax into your surroundings. You know that you are safe, protected and loved, at all times.

You sit down on the grass and allow the sunbeams to warm your body.

In the distance, you notice a swirling vortex of sparkling golden light. It starts moving towards you, yet you feel safe, and also curious about what it could be. Then, before your eyes, a fairy manifests! She holds a golden basket and you can see a cloud of fairy dust surrounding it.

The fairy smiles at you and hands you a piece of paper and a quill pen. She asks you to write down your wish – your heart's desire. She then adds, 'It must be for the highest good of all.'

You take the pen and paper and start to write – about something that is close to your heart, that you would love to see manifested in your life.

As you write, in your mind's eye, you feel what it will feel like when your wish manifests. You allow those feelings to surge through your body, and celebrate as though whatever you have wished for is true right now! Allow yourself some time to really immerse yourself in these feelings.

Then, when you feel ready, you hand the pen and paper back to the fairy, who lowers her golden basket and gestures for you to place the paper upon which your wish is written inside.

As you do this, a puff of fairy dust comes from the basket. Then, hundreds of tiny golden fairies emerge from it holding your wish! They say in unison:

> *Your wish is safe with us, we will take it higher than high,*
> *into the sky, release your wish now, and say goodbye.*
> *Trust in the process, and let us do the rest!*

The fairy with the golden basket smiles and says:

> *Now be open and receptive to the whispers of the fae, we will come to*
> *you in the night or during the day. The inspiration we give comes from*
> *deep in our heart, begin the process now, it is time for you to start.*

The fairy then turns back into a swirling vortex of sparkling light and disappears out of view.

Ground yourself and come fully back into your body.

Once Upon a Time...

This may seem like a strange title for the conclusion of this book. Allow me to explain....

This may be where our journey together ends – at least for the time being. For you, though, this is simply the start of your magical fairy journey.

As I said in this book's Introduction, when working and playing with the fairies, everything is inside out, upside down, back to front and betwixt and between. So, you see, there really are no endings or beginnings where fairies are concerned. As we have learned, time is not linear in Fairyland.

My wish is that you will take what you have gleaned from these pages, and implement this newly discovered knowledge in your own way, as you write your own unique story of connecting with the fae.

It is an honour to have been your human fairy guide as we have explored 111 ways to connect with the fairies.

I wish you love, light and magical fairy blessings as you start your journey into the wonderful world of fairy whispering.

Expect the unexpected, and merrily go with the fairy flow!

Until next time,

Karen Kay

Acknowledgements

Firstly, I would like to thank the fairies, for their love and support and for being a constant source of inspiration and fun (even if it is at 4 o'clock in the morning!).

Thank you to Brian and Wendy Froud, for the magic they bring into the world through their art and knowledge of the fairy realms. I am grateful for the inspiration and support they have given me over the many years I have known them, and for writing the foreword for this book.

I would like to thank Jaye Gould, The Historical Herbalist, for her inspirational research, which informed the Hawthorn Tree Fairy Portals entry.

Huge thanks to Estella Lukas, for her assistance, wisdom and insight in the *Seven-Pointed Fairy (or Elven) Star* and *The Fairy Cities Meditations* entries. To read her in-depth fairy city meditations, see *FAE* magazine (www.faemagazine.com) Issue 6 (Spring 2009), Issue 7 (Summer 2009), Issue 8 (Autumn 2009) and Issue 9 (Winter 2009).

Thank you to all of my friends and family, especially my grandmother who this book is dedicated to. To those who encourage and support me with my fairy mission, including Armorel, Violet, MicheleAnn, Michelle from Cornwall and Danniella Jaine. Extra thanks to my sons, Kailash and Samayan, and their partners who are both called Amy! I love you all!

Last but by no means least, thank you to my Hay House family, for always believing in me, supporting me on my writing journey and for helping me to spread the fairy word! I'm so grateful.

© Danniella Jaine

About the Author

Karen Kay is known as 'The Fairy and Mermaid Whisperer' for her powerful connection to elemental beings. Karen hosts the 3 Wishes Fairy Festival, Fairy Balls and Fayres in Glastonbury, UK, and is the founder and editor-in-chief of *FAE* (Faeries and Enchantment) magazine – both of which celebrate all things fairy.

A passionate nature-lover, Karen's friendship with the fairies began as a young child in her grandmother's garden, where she used to collect rose petals to make perfume for the flower fairies.

🌐 **karenkay.co.uk**
f **@karenkayfairy**
📷 **@karenkayfairy**
♪ **@karenkayfairyofficial**

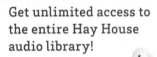

CONNECT WITH

HAY HOUSE

ONLINE

🌐 hayhouse.co.uk   **f** @hayhouse

📷 @hayhouseuk   𝕏 @hayhouseuk

▶ @hayhouseuk   ♪ @hayhouseuk

'*The gateways to wisdom and knowledge
are always open.*'

Louise Hay